Without Shame or Fear

Without Shame or Fear

From Adam to Christ

A. Robert Hirschfeld

Church Publishing
NEW YORK

Unless otherwise noted, the Scripture quotations contained herein are from the New Revised Standard Version Bible, copyright © 1989 by the Division of Christian Education of the National Council of Churches of Christ in the U.S.A. Used by permission. All rights reserved.

Church Publishing
19 East 34th Street
New York, NY 10016
www.churchpublishing.org

Cover image: Masaccio (Maso di San Giovanni) (1401–1428), *Expulsion from Paradise.* 1425–1428. Brancacci Chapel. Photo credit: Eric Lessing / Art Resource, NY.
Cover design by Jennifer Kopec, 2Pug Design
Typeset by Perfectype

Library of Congress Cataloging-in-Publication Data
Names: Hirschfeld, A. Robert, author.
Title: Without shame or fear : from Adam to Christ / A. Robert Hirschfeld.
Description: New York : Church Publishing, 2017.
Identifiers: LCCN 2016040240 (print) | LCCN 2016046108 (ebook) | ISBN 9780819233349 (pbk.) | ISBN 9780819233356 (ebook)
Subjects: LCSH: Shame--Religious aspects--Christianity. | Shame--Biblical teaching.
Classification: LCC BT714 .H57 2017 (print) | LCC BT714 (ebook) | DDC 248.8/6--dc23
LC record available at https://lccn.loc.gov/2016040240

Printed in the United States of America

In Memoriam

Rowan A. Greer III

CONTENTS

INTRODUCTION

You are a child of God. Created by a God whose love cannot be contained, you are a sign of the overflowing and creative goodness of the universe. The world is enhanced by your being in it and will be diminished by your absence. The aim of religion, true religion, is to help you see your unbreakable connection to the God who was, is, and will always be love. This is the mission of Jesus, the Word-made-flesh, who has come into the world, displaying the life that enlightens all people.

> All things came into being through him, and without him not one thing came into being. What has come into being in him was life, and the life was the light of all people. The light shines in the darkness, and the darkness did not overcome it. (John 1:3–5)

What a fine and wondrous thing it would be if that's all we needed to know about the world, about God, and about our relationship to God. But even in those first few exalted and exalting verses of John's Gospel, there is mention of another truth, foreboding and portentous. Darkness competes with the light: in fact, darkness seems to be the primordial condition out of which the light shines and from which the wonder of creation, including our own life and being, emerges.

I am a Christian who needs to rediscover and to be redirected to the Light of Christ that rescues, frees, and saves me from a place where darkness would otherwise overwhelm me. Others may begin the day certain and immediately grateful for the abundant blessings of existence. I need to be reminded, constantly, that I am being created, redeemed, and sustained by God; otherwise, my soul feels disoriented, adrift, forlorn. When I forget God's presence in my life, my soul—the name we might give to that sense of unique identity and self—plummets toward either one of two gravitational abysses: shame or fear.

Shame tells me not only that I have made mistakes that draw me from God's purposes. Shame tells me that *I am* a mistake. The consequence of shame is that one is no longer at home in one's own skin and seeks to hide. In fact, skin and hide are two words whose uses are determined by shame. When free from shame, I am at ease in my own skin—skin is a word that derives from an Old Norse word that means "to shine." Think of what you do with that "little light of yours" when you're feeling no shame. In contrast, hide is the name we give to the tissue that covers certain animals and what our primeval parents are provided after their expulsion from Paradise. After the Fall from grace, finding themselves ashamed for their nakedness, Adam and Eve both hide and manufacture hides out of what's available to them. Rarely do we refer to our skin as our hide, though some may sadly remember being threatened with having our hides "tanned" for having incurred the anger of a parent or guardian.

Shame has been described as a "master emotion," a psychological state that undergirds other emotions such as anger, fear, anxiety, and depression.[1] In that way, shame seems so internalized, such a part of

---

1. For this description of shame as a "master emotion" and for other insights about unacknowledged shame, I am indebted to psychologists Jack Danielian and Patricia Gianotti and their book *Listening with Purpose: Entry Points into Shame and Narcissistic Vulnerability* (Lanham, MD: Jason Aronson, 2012).

our inner landscape that we don't even notice that it's there and that it is churning other responses and reactions to events. Unconscious of shame's capacity to distort our sense of self, we are more vulnerable to messages that confirm that we are lacking. Clearly, we are not immune to the power of idealized images of the human body that seem ideal. Attempts to exploit shame can be seen in the checkout line at the grocery store: magazines with photo-brushed images of men and women present flawless skin and physiques that have the effect of reminding us of our own blemishes, paunches, and wrinkles. Other periodicals work on our sense of lacking by displaying how cluttered and out of date our kitchens and bathrooms are. Some magazines, which tout the value of tidying, simplicity, or even mindfulness, can even work on our shame by telling us how out of sync we are with even our highest values and aspirations.

Why do those yoga practitioners always seem so clear complex-ioned, blissful, and surrounded by such beautiful potted plants on patios overlooking such crystalline babbling brooks? I will be lucky if I get to my rusty and smelly gym locker in between meetings in which I sit too long, eat too much, and drink too much coffee. If I'm feeling less than happy about my condition in life, even less than grateful for being able to purchase sufficient, healthy, and safe food to feed my family, if I'm feeling instead a little blue about my life—I've come to see that my shame, covert and persistent, has been quietly stirred. In this way it works as a "master emotion," a source of emotional power that drives other emotions, even if it doesn't show itself so openly.

Every Advent we hear these words as we approach the altar at the Holy Eucharist:

It is right, and a good and joyful thing, always and everywhere to give thanks to you, Father Almighty, Creator of heaven and earth: Because you sent your beloved Son to redeem us from sin and death, and to make us heirs in him of everlasting life; that when he shall come again in power and great triumph to judge the world, we may *without shame or fear* rejoice to behold his appearing. (Proper Preface for Advent, Book of Common Prayer, 361, 378)

For years I have prayed that prayer, wondering if this would be the Advent when I would be free of shame and fear so that I could really and truly celebrate a glorious Christmas. The prayer says that, because Jesus has already come, has already redeemed us from sin and death and made us fellow heirs of everlasting life, we can fully expect that our shame and fear have *already* been released and dissolved. We no longer have to cower in a defensive crouch when our judge comes. We've had our dignity and worth restored. Already. We don't have to be anxious or fearful or depressed at the approach of the Light that is coming into the world. Shame is not a Christian habit of mind—it is not a virtue to be cultivated or instilled or inflicted on either ourselves or others. We can be free of it. We can rejoice to behold the coming of Jesus and to see his skin radiate with love for us.

But, there it is. That gap, that lack, that coming up short, that missing the mark, that makes me want to hide. There are two truths about the prayers: the first is that the reality they describe has already been accomplished. Sin and death have been defeated in Jesus so that shame and fear may no longer be our "master" emotions. And the second truth is that we find ourselves praying these words again, once more, as though for the first time. As a friend once told me about the need to be converted to the life of grace: this is not a one-walk dog. Shame seems to need to be taken out for a walk a few times a day to do its business. The good news is that grace, God's contradictory love,

God's unreasonable and illogical and infinitely resilient acceptance of us, comes along for the walk as well. Always.

This book is a series of meditations on scenes in Scripture through the particular lens of shame. The purpose is to look directly at shame so that we can see it for what it is—a clinging effect of sin. Shame is the lingering evidence of our having bought the lie that we are unworthy of God's loving regard. As I looked at certain Bible passages where shame seems to figure prominently, almost as a character itself in the stories, I found myself also wondering if there was a positive function to shame. I began to wonder if its persistence in my inner life drives me deeper into a reliance on God's mercy. Adam, Eve, Noah, Ham and Canaan, Sarah, David, the unnamed man blind from birth, and ultimately Jesus himself—all know shame. Jesus shows us how we can be released from shame, so that we can live, love, and serve with a kind of reckless abandon and with dignity, shame's enemy and opposite.

The six chapters that follow focus on passages in the Bible. They contain examples of shame in more contemporary contexts, from my own life, and from the experiences of others. They are not the only passages or verses in the Bible that mention the phenomenon of shame. Quite possibly, a whole book could be written on the subtle differences in how shame is mentioned in the Psalms or on how Paul manages to move from his deep remorse at having been a persecutor of the followers of the way, having held the coats of those who stoned Stephen, to becoming the courageous preacher of God's grace. Shame is not a word that appears in Paul's vocabulary, at least not in referring to himself. There is, of course, this description of how the pull of sin works in him:

So I find it to be a law that when I want to do what is good, evil lies close at hand. For I delight in the law of God in my inmost self, but

I see in my members another law at war with the law of my mind, making me captive to the law of sin that dwells in my members. Wretched man that I am! Who will rescue me from this body of death? Thanks be to God through Jesus Christ our LORD!

So then, with my mind I am a slave to the law of God, but with my flesh I am a slave to the law of sin. (Romans 7:21–25)

If we accept that shame asserts that we not only sin, but also that we are, in essence and in body, a sin, unworthy and repugnant to God, then it doesn't take very long—one verse—for the apostle to get out of shame's psychic trap. That's a kind of spiritual *chutzpah* I've longed and prayed for but struggle to attain. I admire it when I see such audacity in people who apply their spiritual confidence (literally, their "with-faith-ness") to the work of protecting and enhancing the dignity of others or to the health and protection of the planet. While I am often weighed down by the timid encrustation of shame, I admire how others so shine with a radiance of God's fire of love and desire for justice. Imagine the social and cultural advances we would now be deprived of had Jackie Robinson, Rosa Parks, or Martin Luther King Jr. accepted the shame that the dominant culture strove to instill in them. How their families and churches turned shame into dignity for the benefit, not only of them personally, but of the whole society, is what makes, in my mind, their biographies so riveting. One hope for this book is that it will stir conversations in small groups about how our Church can move out of its shell of self-consciousness, its long-standing obsession with its reputation and need to keep up appearances, and adopt a holy shamelessness. Such was the attitude of our Savior, gently yet boldly demonstrated in the Upper Room on the night before he suffered, and gloriously displayed on the cross.

I find that it's difficult to discuss shame without looking at images and telling stories, and so I rely on depictions of the human face and bodies rendered in art, cinema, and in my own life. Our faith celebrates the truth that God became human flesh so that human flesh can share in the glorious freedom of God. When examining shame, entering into its complicated and barbed meanings in our life, it becomes clear that one reason why the Word was made flesh is that shame is felt in our bodies. It distorts our vision, makes us physically cringe and wince. We experience shame in our flesh. It alters how we approach a mirror, our neighbor, and our God.

The mission of God—from the Creation, to the Incarnation, to the Passion, to the Resurrection and the Ascension—is to transform our experience of shame into the glory of God and so to make us alive in Jesus. We are meant to reign with God in this life and the next. In my experience, it is shame that is the roadblock in the highway to that heaven. My hope is that this small book will help us share in that mission without shame or fear so that we may rejoice to behold Christ's appearing now and when he comes again in glory.

1

Christmas Trees and Fig Leaves

Then the eyes of both were opened, and they knew that they were naked; and they sewed fig leaves together and made loincloths for themselves. They heard the sound of the LORD God walking in the garden at the time of the evening breeze, and the man and his wife hid themselves from the presence of the LORD God among the trees of the garden.

—Genesis 3:7–8

Every year the Christmas trees travel down the highway from Canada in large trucks. The trees look like needles with their branches folded up and wrapped in nylon netting. I usually see the first truckload a week or so before Thanksgiving while I am traveling from parish to parish throughout the Diocese of New Hampshire. I must admit that the first feeling I have is very far from the excitement and glee I remember feeling as a little boy. Then, my sister and I, upon seeing the first sign of an open Christmas tree lot or the first colored lights festooning a house or a shrub in our suburban Minneapolis neighborhood, would giggle with excitement for Christmas and begin the countdown of days. It was the glow of the season that captured me, even more than the hope of a new bicycle, sled, or chemistry set. What made Christmas special was the sense of being in the presence of the holy, which back then was conveyed to me, believe it or not, by the particular way red and blue and green lights would reflect off white snow. That glow would give enough light for me to aim my sled toward the bottom of the run in my neighbor's backyard. It's hard to conceive how stringing lights on the evergreen trees in the yard was all it took to convey to me the presence of God, a presence that I could enjoy for hours in the dark and the cold. That's all it took: colored lights on Christmas trees.

Nowadays it's different. I'm middle age, middle class, with debts, mortgages, college tuitions, a cramped schedule, lists of chores and shopping, and difficult conversations to negotiate. Seeing a Christmas tree can bring with it a certain sense of gloom, of portent: I won't be able to fit it all in. I won't be able to afford what's asked of me, either emotionally or financially. Add to this that sighting a Christmas tree or hearing Christmas carols at the local supermarket shortly after Halloween brings the sense that time has slipped by once again, a whole year, and what is there to show for it? Far from the childhood glee and exhilaration, the dread that a Christmas tree incurs is real.

After some reflection, I have discovered that the annual feeling that the Christmas tree stirs in me is more existential than just the seasonal blues or the SAD—Seasonal Affective Disorder—that can come with a northern winter. Perverse as it may seem to the consumer-driven

Christmas industry that bids our hearts be cheery, I have come to the conclusion that contemplation on the origin of the old Tannenbaum can bring us to remember the experience of shame. Acknowledging the dynamic of shame may remind us of how our having fallen out of God's warm glow has been met with the restorative infusion of love in God's taking on our flesh in Jesus, the event we await in Advent.

To see how this works will require us to go back to the events that took place, as the Creation story goes, around the Paradise Tree in the Garden of Eden. It is not very well known, far less celebrated, that December 24 is the Feast Day of Adam and Eve. Rarely seen as deserving veneration, these two are in a sense exiled from the family history of humanity for having disobeyed God in the Garden and for introducing sin into the mix. But on the eve of Christmas, their exile is lifted, and they, along with the Paradise Tree, which is the object of their temptation, are allowed to come into our homes. It doesn't take too much imagination to see how the brightly colored glass bulbs hanging from our fir trees resemble the fruit that was forbidden.

Paradise

Let's go back to that first story in our family history. If one searches the opening three chapters of Genesis looking for some indication of what it was like for Adam and Eve to be in that blessed state before the Fall, one might be surprised at how little we can say. Any emotional and psychological descriptions of that blessed state are absent. We can infer that they are in a state of bliss and contentment, but there is really no explicit indication that they are, in fact, happy. The best clue that we can take of some positive feeling from either of them comes from Adam upon his introduction to Eve after he wakes from that mysterious divine anesthesia needed for the extraction of his rib. "Then the man said, 'This at last is bone of my bones and flesh of my flesh . . .'" (Genesis 2:23a). This "at last" would indicate some relief at no longer having to tend the Garden alone. It's as though Adam is saying, "Finally, after all this time, I have someone to talk to who can understand me because she shares what it means to have flesh like mine!" But even that might be a projection, an insertion of our own experience, into the Bible passage. Again, the Scripture is quite silent about the inner life of our spiritual ancestors. The only thing we can say for certain, based on what the Bible actually says, is found in the following verses: "And the man and his wife were both naked, and were not ashamed" (Genesis 2:25).

It's startling when one thinks of it, really. After all, though the word is actually not used in Genesis, we have come to describe the Garden of Eden as paradise and to think of it as a time and place as close to heaven on earth as we have ever come. This is in the days before poverty, racism, hunger, war, and every other kind of depredation. But the closest we get to a description of what we have come to believe was the bliss before the Fall is that they are not ashamed. Upon first realizing this, one might feel a sense of deep betrayal by the Bible. Part of us might want to say, "What the heck, Holy Writ? Is that all you can say about what it was like for Adam and Eve when they had everything going for them? No expressions of ecstatic happiness? No songs of mirth and exuberance? All you can say is that they were not ashamed?"

It's safe to say that western culture is keenly interested in the inner life. From the self-disclosive *Confessions* of Augustine, to the "confessional" poets of the twentieth century, to the courageously revealing spiritual writings of Anne Lamott (just to name a few), we are interested in what's going on in the human heart. We read these writers with interest partly because we need some reassurance that we are not alone in our struggles in life. But Scripture is often reticent when it comes to the interior world. And so it might be striking that the state of mind of Adam and Eve is not of much interest to the Scripture writers, except by their having registered the absence of a feeling that is so deeply rooted in the human experience—that of shame.

Could it be that our modern interests, or some might say even obsession, in personal fulfillment or purpose, in the avoidance of depression or anxiety—none of which are mentioned by name in the Scriptures—all boil down to the experience of shame? Though we pine for the days of unmitigated bliss that we project onto our dear spiritual ancestors Adam and Eve, the Bible actually doesn't ascribe any other emotion to them besides the absence of shame. Some in my (baby boomer) generation may remember the nostalgic anthem sung after the great "Festival of Peace and Music," better known as Woodstock. As the song went, "We gotta get back to the garden!" as though the lack of porta-potties, the mud, the drugs, the lack of food and water, and the unreported sexual assaults and humiliation that took place in those fields in Upstate New York somehow realized the Edenic ideal. Projection and denial are powerful things.

Disobedience and Awareness

After eating from the fruit of the tree of the knowledge of good and evil, the eyes of Adam and Eve are opened,

> . . . and they knew that they were naked; and they sewed fig leaves together and made loincloths for themselves. They heard the sound of the LORD God walking in the garden at the time of the evening . . . (Genesis 3:7–8)

The story is called an etiology; that is, it serves to explain or give a reason for a condition. Woven into the human condition is the experience of shame. To be a human being means to feel shame. The biblical author of this part of the creation story seems to be offering an answer to the pervasive and inescapable feeling that makes us want to hide from our God and our neighbor. After partaking of the fruit of the tree that was forbidden them, they suddenly are made aware of themselves and their vision is made clear about their condition of nakedness.

To use the language that theologians have adopted, they fall from a state of grace, which seems to be akin to a state of ignorance. The awareness of themselves as naked coincides with the knowledge of having disobeyed God. The effect of the disobedience is a sudden vision of themselves *in comparison* to their fellow creature and certainly to God. Whereas, previous to the serpent's temptation, there was no hint that they were separate from God, now they recognize that God is *out there somewhere, lurking.*

At the sound of God walking in the garden at the time of the evening breeze, Adam and Eve panic and run to hide among the other trees in the garden, revealing their awareness of God's judgment and their separateness, even before God expresses disappointment and judgment upon them. Adam and Eve recognize their fall prior to God's stern encounter with them. Their creatureliness—having been created by a creator whom they are not—puts them in a disfavored state and results in their shame. Seeing themselves as naked is seeing themselves as creatures of God, as having been formed of one who is infinitely greater, more powerful, *infinitely more* than who they are. Adam and Eve come upon this feeling all on their own, before God asks them anything about why they are wearing clothes or why they are lurking behind trees, and before God has expressed displeasure for their having trespassed the commandment not to eat of the fruit of the tree.

The Inner Mind

Teachers of Buddhist meditation and mindfulness sometimes refer to the plight of the "comparison mind"—the habit we all have of rating ourselves for better or worse in relation to others. When did you first reckon with the truth that you didn't run as fast as your sibling, or were not as quick in mathematics as your classmate? And, conversely, when did you first derive a sense of comfort from realizing that you lived in a more stylish and expensive part of town than others, or that your parents' car was nicer than the cluttered minivan of your friends?

If we are honest, we know that such comparisons are silently going on in our minds all the time. Our minds are busy making comparisons even while we are sitting in our pews in church: "Who gets to sit up there next to the altar?" "I could read that text from Ezekiel far better than he did!" Or, perhaps even more often, "I am not as put together as the people in this congregation. Compared to all these saints, my life is a complete wreck. What right do I have to be here? Please, God, don't make me have to say anything to anyone. Let me just sit here and pray. Maybe then I can get out of here safely without being revealed for the fraud and scoundrel that I really am!"

The framers of the Book of Common Prayer seem to have taken all this mental static into account when they chose to open the liturgy of the Holy Eucharist with the prayer that is known as the Collect for Purity:

> Almighty God, to you all hearts are open, all desires known, and
> from you no secrets are hid: Cleanse the thoughts of our hearts by

the inspiration of your Holy Spirit, that we may perfectly love you, and worthily magnify your holy Name; through Jesus Christ our Lord. (BCP, 355)

I notice it is becoming more common in the churches that I visit to adopt the practice of inviting the whole congregation to pray the words of this prayer, instead of just the priest. In doing so, it's as though we all move out from our cover behind the trees, where Adam and Eve sought hiding, and we risk allowing ourselves to be open to the One who already knows what is in the recesses of our hearts and our memories.

The passage in Genesis does not dwell on the emotional trauma that accrues to Adam and Eve upon their realization that they are not God and that in each other's presence they would need to cover themselves in order not to be seen as insufficient in their nakedness. There are very few monologues in the Scriptures where a character benefits from an aside, like in Shakespeare when the action of the play pauses to allow the character to reveal the inner workings, doubts and quandaries, or strategy making. However, that reticence of the Scriptures does not prevent us from pausing in our reading to imagine the inner life of the figures we meet there who, over a lifetime of prayer and reflection, become in a real sense part of our own life stories, dwelling in our inner life.

Adam and Eve are a gift of the Scriptures to us. When we read about them, we are actually reading about ourselves, and each time we encounter them, another facet of their story comes to light. Just like when we look at a family photo album and new information is often revealed to the viewer, even though the photograph itself does not change from year to year. We change, and often the people with whom we are turning the pages of the album are not the same. New stories are told and new truths are disclosed in a small detail that is noticed or shared for the first time. Adam and Eve occupy a page or two in our family album over which it is profitable to pause and reflect. What must have been going through their minds as they punctured the holes in the fig leaves to sew those britches together? I imagine that it was not a shared task, but that each went behind their own tree to learn how to accomplish this chore apart. That is certainly one sorry effect of shame: isolation. Although they had been charged with the stewardship and tending of the garden in the beginning, it probably did not feel like doing chores, but sewing fig leaves together could very well represent the dreadful introduction of drudgery.

Samuel Beckett and O

When sitting at the family album of Scripture contemplating Adam and Eve at the painful moment that their eyes are opened, I find myself alongside one of the most penetrating poets and playwrights of the twentieth century, Samuel Beckett, who offers insight into what happened at that pivotal moment in human consciousness. In his only foray into cinema, Beckett dramatized the terrible burden of the self's need to hide from any observer, whether that observer be a neighbor, God, or even one's own self. Though not alluding directly to the story in Genesis, Film[2] gets to the emotionally complex texture of shame and self-consciousness that would not, I suspect, be far from what the inspired Scripture writer had in mind. One can see in the age-weathered face of the silent film star Buster Keaton the fear and the shame that compel his character, known simply in the screenplay as O (for object), to protect his one field of vision from seeing any other eye, including the eye of the camera, referred to in the script as E.

---

2. You can see a short clip here: www.youtube.com/watch?v=4_Esx3oAR6I.

The simple plot involves Keaton's O doing all he can to keep himself from being perceived. Beckett uses the sparse format of his screenplay to dramatize the proposition of the seventeenth-century philosopher and Anglican priest George Berkeley that *esse est percipi*; that is, to be is to be perceived. To state it more fully, our existence relies on our being seen, and our being seen in essence determines our existence. It was this proposition that led to countless late-night college bull sessions around the question: if a tree falls in the woods without anyone there to hear or see it fall, did it actually fall? Berkeley postulated that even if no creature witnessed the falling timber, the omnipresent and omniscient God in whom all things have their being is there, providing the requisite "seeing" conditions necessary to the falling tree's existence.

In Beckett's film, the primary character O seeks to avoid the agony of being known. *Film* is essentially a chase flick. O's frantic hiding within the crumbling urban landscape, his scurrying away from any observer, could be exactly what Adam and Eve do among the trees of the Garden, no longer a Paradise. They seem to being running away from anyone who can possibly see them, including themselves. In fact, both the first and last frame of Beckett's short movie is the rather discomforting image of Buster Keaton's eyelid opening. We stare into the dark abyss contained within his iris. It's a threatening image, perhaps for the same reason that the Collect for Purity may initially be threatening to someone worshipping in an Episcopal service for the first time: no secrets are hid.

Potential threats to O in *Film* include: a clergyman, a woman encountered on the street, a picture of a Near-Eastern deity identified in the script as "God the Father," a parakeet, a goldfish, a dog, a cat, O's own reflection in a window and in a mirror, and a pair of ovals resembling eyes that are carved into the backrest of a chair. All these perceptions are horrific to O because to be seen is to be confronted with the terror of being itself. Even photographs of himself as a child on his mother's lap, as a student, and as a groom are all intolerable reminders of an unreconciled and tainted past. The film ends with O having failed to avoid confronting this scrutiny of him, by himself. The divided self longs to cover one's eyes and to be blinded from any awareness of memory, self, or presence. To be perceived is not only to be, but it is being itself that is a terrible thing when shame and fear are so acute.

Self-Discovery

Beckett's short movie is, of course, an overstatement of the feeling of shame and the fear of being discovered, even by one's self. It's a caricature of shame and fear and seems dated to the heyday of existentialism when people relished in absurd drama, smoked French cigarettes, and wore black turtlenecks. But watching Keaton's performance, in the light of the Genesis account of the eye opening of Adam and Eve, causes me to remember those times in my life when even the prospect of being seen horrified me. Once, while driving in the car with me and passing a local high school at the end of the school day, my daughter, not far in age from being a teenager herself, remarked, "It's an awful time. I feel so bad for them. You don't even want to be in your own skin." Of course, such a statement, said in confidence between family members when sweeping generalizations are permissible, is probably not universally true, but it did speak to her compassion for the American adolescent and the agonizing scrutiny that many feel. This horrifying scrutiny could be dramatized as easily by a teenager as it was by the aging Buster Keaton. Like teenagers, Adam and Eve are not comfortable in their own skin and so they are compelled to manufacture new skins for themselves.

I have access to this feeling. As a teenager I was stricken with acne. Not knowing how it was caused or inflamed, it seemed to appear on my face with suddenness similar to the startling fall of Adam and Eve. As I recall, I was not the first to notice the pimples and purple blemishes on my cheeks and forehead. The awareness of being afflicted, of having to pay attention to my appearance, came to me when someone at the school bus stop greeted me in the morning with, "Wow. You got zits." I can recall the scalding humiliation pouring over my scalp, and my first response was the urge to hide. Simultaneous with that feeling was the unmistakable perception that the relationship I had previously enjoyed with my schoolmate was now one of accusation and finger pointing.

The carefree days of riding a bike together and exploring the ponds and woods in our as yet undeveloped landscape instantly evaporated. It wasn't clear who was at fault. My first reaction was that the appearance of my pimples was the offense, that I had insulted my friend. It may sound strange, but I confess that it took a long time to come to understand that that encounter, in which I came to see myself as a flawed human being, was not about what I had done but was rather a moment of entering, falling, into an awareness of the human condition. A healthier ego, a more robust and guarded self-esteem, may have decided to return the remark about the zits with something equally stinging. Later in my adolescence, I confess, I returned such comments with more than words, resorting even to physical violence. Looking back, those ugly encounters only exacerbated my sense of isolation, of there being an iron wedge between me and my friend. We've never recovered.

Eyes Wide Open

This small story raises more complications. My skin eventually changed and returned. But the shaming of others based on their complexion continues, in fact flares up repeatedly in our nation. I am a white, middle-class, and privileged heterosexual male of western European descent. Though it is not easy speaking about it, it's clear to me and many others that these attributes contributed to my being elected to serve in a place of some power in The Episcopal Church. After one session of the "Meet and Greet" events when candidates for bishop are taken around the diocese to make statements and answer questions about their potential episcopacies, one gentleman approached me to ask who shined my black shoes. When I told him I shined my own shoes, he expressed his approval of me as "a regular guy." I was the only straight male on the slate of nominees that would follow Bishop Gene Robinson, the first openly gay man to be elected as a bishop. As of this writing, out of 131 active bishops in The Episcopal Church's House of Bishops, only eleven are women. Though the demographics of our nation will soon find that people who look and speak like me will be in the minority, the leadership of our church is still, by a wide margin, made up of predominantly white males.

What does shame have to do with these statistics? I would describe it as a pall that is cast on all of us, an undifferentiated feeling that not only is there something awry in the system that advances certain persons to positions of authority, but we ourselves are awry for operating within that system. This sense is real, and though therapists, spiritual directors, coaches, and consultants will urge me to let go of my guilt and to pay little if any heed to that feeling, I have come to realize that such a denial is ultimately self-serving and perpetuates the fantasy that the ground on which we all are playing is even. Unlike the persistent, though eventually treatable, case of acne, the fact that I am granted a significant advantage in this society is not easily erased or mitigated. On the surface my privilege, derived from a "winning" roll of the genetic and ethnic dice, would be the cause for dignity, a sense of worth and a sense of being wholly accepted and honored in the eyes of others and God.

On the other hand, there are moments when, akin to the revelation of Adam and Eve, my eyes are opened and I am brought in close contact with the reality that I am undeserving of many of the benefits I enjoy. If shame brings with it a sense of unworthiness, of being deficient in the eyes of others, then its opposite could be dignity, an attribute Episcopalians promise in our baptismal vows to uphold in every human being. My life in the Christian community has made me aware of how the color of my skin, my gender, my marital status—to name a few of my personal attributes—provide me with advantages in both American society and the Church. Those advantages represent my privilege, my access to power that many others do not automatically have. The injustice of this imbalance is a source of shame. The "dignity of every human being" that we vow to uphold in our baptismal promises is not the same as one's undeserved privilege.

Recent headlines of shootings by white police of unarmed black men, of women being subjugated to sexual exploitation at the hands of men, of unequal pay between men and women, of institutional hatred directed at those who are not of the dominant race or culture or religious heritage of our society—all spur in me a sense of shame, an awareness of participating in a human race whose bond with God and each other is fractured. This is the power of the story of Adam and Eve;

the account of their fall helps us understand that we share the effect of their disobedience and their sin.

Shame and Guilt

It's here that it would be helpful to make a distinction between shame and guilt. Though I may not be guilty of racially motivated hatred and violence, though I have not condoned sexual exploitation of the defenseless, though I have not espoused hatred against adherents of another religion, my sense of shame is distinguishable from being able to say that I am morally without blame. Though we may not be guilty, we still carry the sense of shame. In a sense, shame runs deeper and is more diffuse than guilt.

Though guilt and shame are no doubt related, I'm not sure how I would fill a Venn diagram to illustrate their relationship. Remorse that stems from guilt says, "I have sinned in a particular way and bear responsibility for the trespass. The guilt for this action is mine, and, even though I may have committed the action with accomplices, I did it, and I feel sorry for having offended and committing the harm." Shame, on the other hand, feels to me more tectonic, and by that I mean it underlies and provides the energy for the sins that may occur in an individual. Occasionally, even in a geologically quiet place like New Hampshire, the sudden awareness that there are dynamics underneath our feet, over which we have no control or influence, jolts us. A minor quake makes us aware of these powers. Shame can work this way—its energy is hidden, lying below the surface of our day-to-day awareness. But an occasion of sin may cause it to erupt, in the same way that an earthquake felt on the earth's crust is the result of forces at play down below. When we commit a particular sin and are confronted about it, there are times when our remorse is so severe that it exceeds the scale of an offense. In those moments, it could be that deeper forces are being unleashed.

An example could be found in the account of the fall of Adam and Eve itself. For many readers, the punishment meted out by God is preposterous and indicates the arbitrary meanness of a temperamental God. Such severe punishment is, after all, for what—the purloining of a piece of fruit? Eternal banishment for tasting something God probably knew was very tempting? Who is really at fault here? Those who've read St. Augustine's *Confessions,* perhaps the first spiritual autobiography of western civilization, will note that despite committing what we moderns would consider utterly selfish and abominable acts—sexual promiscuity, abandonment of partner and children, intellectual arrogance—it's not any of these things that give him a sense of moral unease. What tips him over the edge and drives him to seek the forgiveness with God? The stealing of a pear! It's this relatively—no, ridiculously—minor offense that sparks the emotional tremor within Augustine that leads him to conversion to Christ and, one could argue, the reams of pages that became his literary legacy (all while functioning as a bishop, no less). For some, shame debilitates, paralyzing all action. For others, like Augustine, for instance, it seems to motivate.

Original Sin

It's therefore fitting that Augustine is attributed with developing one of the most complicated doctrines of the Church, that of "original sin." This doctrine says that the sin of Adam and Eve, their disobedience in the Garden, is transmitted and spread, contaminating all humanity as though it is a hereditary disease. According to the words of the Articles of Religion,[3] original sin, or birth-sin, is an "infection of [human] nature" that remains "in every person born into this world." Many, including myself, struggle with the doctrine of original sin so described on a number of levels. It tends to locate the awareness of my human limitation—the fact that I am not God and that I am flawed and tend toward gratifying selfish desires—to the physical realm. Original sin is the reason why the "flesh lusteth contrary to the Spirit." Not surprisingly, therefore, most people who were introduced to the concept of original sin associate it with sex. Adam and Eve saw each other as naked as a result of their disobedience, and the shame that is introduced is primarily the result of their carnality or of their lust. It's a physical thing. When understood this way, original sin as a teaching of the church, and the shame it can spur, can be used as a means of tainting any kind of sexual attraction that is not within the purposes set forth by certain religious authorities, many of whom have devoted themselves, at least publically, to lives of celibacy.

When seen as an infection of the flesh, the doctrine of original sin doesn't offer an understanding of us beyond our own individual collection of bodily organs and desires. When original sin, at least in the popular imagination and understanding, is seen only in terms of the desires of the flesh, we are less likely to look at the phenomena of racism, misogyny, pride, fear and hatred of other ethnicities and religions, greed, envy, and all the rest of the full catastrophe of the human condition as connected to the experience of the very first human beings until the present day. I am more attracted to the doctrine of original

---

3. Book of Common Prayer, 869.

sin when I see it as an attempt, albeit flawed, to describe what we all know is true: humanity, with rare exception, tends to mess things up, royally, and I share that condition. As a man of privilege, with eyes open to the ways I have benefited from the disorder of God's creation, I know I have a responsibility to be aware of my advantage and to do what I can to mitigate, with God's help, the suffering of others. I often fail in this task.

It is with this awareness each year that I pull down the box containing the tree stand, the string of lights, the glass bulbs with their bent paperclip hangers, and the kindly angel to prepare another Paradise Tree. Happily, the angel that I perch on the top won't be wielding a sword of flame to banish my family and me out of the garden of our family room. Instead, she looks rather kindly, with her crimson hoop skirt and the plastic candle with its tiny white lightbulb. Though technically angels are of indeterminate gender, the one on top of our tree, bought for all of five dollars at a St. Nicholas Fair at the last parish I served, reminds me of that reflected glow on the snow-covered hill in my neighbor's yard outside Minneapolis. The angel's eyes are open to my life, to "the hope and fears of all the years" that have transpired since that time of relative innocence when I could sled all night before my mother called my sister and me in to get ready for bed. My sister is no longer with us, and the years since then have shown me a measured share of suffering and sin, much of which I caused myself. Adam is in me after all. With her ruddy cheeks reflecting the varied hues of the tree lights, the angel's eyes are open, but they are not staring at me to accuse or condemn. Her open eyes, which follow me no matter where I wander around the room, tell me that this is a tree behind which there is no need to hide.

Questions for Reflection or Discussion

- Consider the story of Adam and Eve before and after the Fall, from when they were not ashamed to the moment when they seek to hide. Are there such "before and after" moments in your life?

- How do you interpret the Church's teaching that all human-kind is created in the image of God? What does that image look like to you?

- How much time and energy do you spend comparing yourself to an image of yourself that is either flawless or damaged? Who created those images of yourself? God? Or someone else?

- How might you invite Adam and Eve, forgiven and thoroughly loved by God, into your Christmas celebration? How might they change how you approach the busy-ness of Christmas?

2

The Nakedness of Noah

Noah, a man of the soil, was the first to plant a vineyard. He drank some of the wine and became drunk, and he lay uncovered in his tent. And Ham, the father of Canaan, saw the nakedness of his father, and told his two brothers outside. Then Shem and Japheth took a garment, laid it on both their shoulders, and walked backward and covered the nakedness of their father; their faces were turned away, and they did not see their father's nakedness.

—Genesis 9:20–23

Tucked in the pages of Genesis is a tiny but unsettling story of Noah and his son Ham who "uncovers the nakedness of his father." Again, the account is an etiology, a story that functions to explain how things are and how they got to be that way. Without going to the Bible commentaries and the biblical scholars, it might be hard at first glance to guess what questions this story is trying to answer.

Here are some of my guesses: Where did the Canaanites (descendants of Ham) come from and what explains the age-old hostility between them and other descendants of Noah? What is the source and reason for the extreme uneasiness one feels when contemplating the sexuality of one's parents or close relations? Why do we need to protect the vulnerability of those who are weaker than we are, whether that weakness includes not merely physical weaknesses, but also moral flaws?

The extent to which Shem and Japheth go to prevent themselves from seeing what Ham sees, the genitals of their father Noah, seems to demand ingenuity on their part. One can imagine wondering how they came upon and agreed to the strategy of taking a garment, laying it upon their shoulders, and walking backward, all the while making sure that they were looking away. How did they keep from stumbling on a rock or a log while walking backward? More importantly, what in them gave them such an urgent need to protect their father in his vulnerability, in his exposure, even when he was in the privacy of his own tent?

Nakedness

Preachers who are bound to the Revised Common Lectionary might be grateful to its compilers that this passage does not appear as one of the selections for any of the Sunday mornings in the church year. We are naturally reluctant to venture into those areas of our life that are meant to be private. We now have a code for signaling when a conversation is moving into territory that might be akin to that which Ham seems to have stumbled upon: T.M.I. stands for "Too Much Information." Often when I've heard a person employ those initials, they actually raise their hand to their eyes or their ears as if to protect themselves from witnessing more than what they deem appropriate.

One might wonder what Ham actually saw that would have so outraged his father. Was it simply the fact that he was inebriated? Most likely Ham stumbled upon more than the sight of his drunken father dancing around his tent with the equivalent of a Paleolithic or Iron-Age lampshade on his head. A search of the Bible for the word "nakedness" reveals some other possibilities that would definitely fall under the category of T.M.I. According to Leviticus:

> None of you shall approach anyone near of kin to uncover nakedness: I am the LORD. You shall not uncover the nakedness of your father, which is the nakedness of your mother; she is your mother, you shall not uncover her nakedness. You shall not uncover the nakedness of your father's wife; it is the nakedness of your father. You shall not uncover the nakedness of your sister, your father's daughter or your mother's daughter, whether born at home or born abroad. You shall not uncover the nakedness of your son's daughter or of your daughter's daughter, for their nakedness is your own nakedness. (Leviticus 18:6–10)

One notices the transitive nature of nakedness. The nakedness of the mother is also the nakedness of the father and *vice versa*. It's possible that what Ham saw was not only the nakedness of Noah, but also the unnamed wife of Noah, whose nakedness was not merely her own, but Noah's as well. In other words, it could be that Ham, the more inquisitive, precocious youngest child, heard noises coming from the tent and decided to investigate. Not knowing that it was taboo, he then reported what he saw to his older brothers, Shem and Japheth, who, as older siblings often do, had a more developed sense of what was inappropriate. The older brothers chose to protect their father, perhaps even his wife, from being vulnerable to further exposure. They took it as their family duty to cover Noah.

In this way, they seem to act out of a similar impulse as Adam and Eve when they knit together the loincloths out of the fig leaves. There is something in us, the Bible seems to say, that instinctively knows that certain things need to be covered up and kept to ourselves, protected. Otherwise, when certain matters are exposed, they become a source of shame. Prudish preachers—and I would count myself in that number—can consider themselves fortunate that the framers of the lectionary themselves actually do the same work as Shem and Japheth by excluding this passage from worship, in effect covering over the passage so that tender ears don't have to imagine the possibilities within Noah's tent. There's no need to spark voyeurism on a Sunday morning, even if it is given full reign during prime time. But let's return to that later.

Punishment

As Ham and his son Canaan—an innocent bystander—learn, the consequence of uncovering Noah's shame is beyond severe. In fact, one would have to say that the punishment of Canaan for an offense that would be more fittingly applied to his father seems utterly inordinate and unjust. Why would Ham's son, a lad who, according to the account in Genesis, had nothing to do with Ham's supposed offense, be punished with a lifetime of abject slavery? How can Noah's curse of his own grandchild be justified? The Scripture itself seems to beg that question and to invite us to argue with Noah's disproportionate "morning-after" reaction. Canaan is not only the unwitting individual recipient of Noah's ire but is also an archetypal figure whose name comes to stand for a whole people.

Canaan is the name given to those who will be conquered in the pursuit of a promised land; Canaanites are those who, in later accounts, must be driven out so that Israel can receive the Promised Land. Thus, as in etiology, a narrative account that serves to explain a condition present at the time of the story's writing, we surmise that it at least partly answers the questions, "What accounts for the plight of the Canaanites?" and "To what do they owe their abject status?" The account of Noah's curse suggests that the original condemnation of Canaan is to be passed on from one generation to another in an unbroken chain of transmission. Rather than presenting it as a simple transgression for which there can be made a satisfactory punishment or restitution, Canaan must carry a condition that is not so simply rectified: shame.

It all speaks, I suspect, to the capacity of shame itself to spread beyond and over any reason. As we saw in the account of Adam and Eve, shame is the awareness of one's unworthiness in the sight of God. Quite possibly, the Bible writers seek to implicate shame as at least part of the justification for Israel's overtaking by force of the land it is promised after the Exodus from Egypt and the wandering in the desert. The story of Canaan functions also as a strong caution to those who may be tempted to transgress sexual taboos within close family relations. Vigilant protection of these relationships is absolutely necessary not only for the proper health of each member of the whole community, but also for the prosperity of the whole nation.

Human Dignity

Since the lectionary "covers up" this whole uncomfortable story, we can avoid in-depth investigations about its meaning in sermons on Sunday morning. It would seem quite self-evident that there are things about our family members' "nakedness," however imagined, that are to remain undisclosed and safely shuttered from view. Each time we in

The Episcopal Church renew our own baptismal vows, we pledge "to uphold the dignity of every human being." One would think that being scrupulous to honor one another's privacy would be a basic, assumed condition of honoring human dignity. As we believe that baptism initiates all people to a relationship of kinship with one another in God, the rule against looking at another's nakedness applies not only to one's own immediate family, not only to the household of faith, but indeed to all humankind. "Every human being" in the baptismal liturgy means *every* human being. The story of Noah and his sons tells us that the consequences of not upholding the dignity of our sisters and brothers contribute greatly beyond whatever happens around one's personal tent.

That the story might make us cringe speaks to the power of its claim on us. This seems obvious. Who would want to venture into the metaphorical tent in the way that Ham does? Even if he did stumble unwittingly upon the "nakedness" of Noah, it could very well be that what's punishable is his choice to announce what he saw to his brothers rather than immediately to avert his eyes and be silent. His publishing of the indignity could be as much the sin and cause of shame as the fact that he saw something that he should not have.

Schadenfreude

Actually, we might want to consider this story in our communities of faith more than we do. At first I wondered what this story could possibly have to say about our modern-day culture. We all know not to peek where we shouldn't, don't we? Don't we all have doors that we can close to keep our children, houseguests, and even our spouses from seeing our "nakedness" at certain prescribed moments in our day-to-day life?

The story of Ham and Canaan, we might like to think, speaks to things that are so obvious about human interactions, why even bring it up? Of course it's not read in public. We are all fully aware of appropriate boundaries when it comes to protecting our closest relations from such exposure. Who needs to be cautioned by reading the cringe-making story about the sin of Ham and the curse of Canaan?

But then I went to the local YMCA in the middle of the day and climbed onto one of the exercise machines, joining about a dozen other people of various ages, all pointed in the same direction to begin our respective routines of excursion and hard breathing and sweat. At the front of the "Cardio Room" and hanging from the ceiling at various latitudes are a score of television screens. Some display the sports channel, some a variety of news media, but most are tuned to a daytime talk show that features men and women who, in front of a live audience, are being interviewed about all kinds of transgressions against each other. Some involve intimate liaisons with adult stepchildren, former spouses, coworkers, or former classmates encountered at school reunions. On occasion the announcement of a spouse's infidelity is made for the first time on the set of the television studio, or so it is designed to appear. The host of the program coaxes the confessions out of these seemingly ordinary individuals with a feigned shock and incredulity, as though he is the standard-bearer for moral propriety who, day by day, is astounded by the unlimited variety of perversity. When a husband or wife learns for the first time of a spouse's repeated infidelity with a close and trusted friend, outbursts of tears and rage result. At this point, the demeanor of the show's host shifts between that of a patient and compassionate pastor to a referee at a professional wrestling match.

All the while, the cameras pan to the live audience. The people feel utterly free to shout out their disgust at the disclosures onstage.

At one moment they groan in sympathy at the heartbreak of a woman whose husband is revealed to be a sex addict, only to shout in revulsion at the same woman when it is revealed, after returning from the commercial break for an advertisement for air freshener, that she has been "sexting" nude photos of herself over the internet. The audience simultaneously shudders in disbelief and laughs. They seem enthralled by the entertainment.

Meanwhile, back at the YMCA, on the opposite coast of the nation from where all this is being filmed, it's as though, like Ham, we just stumbled onto a scene that we did not choose. The television screens pour out all this suffering and, if we are disgusted by it, still no one gets up to turn the switch off or to change the channel. Some of us pretend we are too engrossed in our labors on the StairMaster, or the Concept2 rowing machine, or the stationary bicycles, to care. That is the excuse I've hidden behind when these programs are on. I pretend that the viewing of what's going on in my neighbors' tent has no effect on me and that it doesn't sink into or distort my invulnerable and clean soul. But the fact is, here I am, remembering these scenes with some revulsion, sadness, remorse even, for having participated in the entertainment of uncovering and relishing in the indignity of another. Their shame seems to have fallen on me. Though I did not choose that channel, I didn't shut it off either. Perhaps because I was unwilling to risk offending the fellow on the stationary bike next to me if he was actually enjoying the program—was it helping him get through his last few miles to nowhere? Or was I simply unwilling to disrupt my own workout? For whatever reason, I left the cardio room feeling something like the curse of Ham. I needed a shower, not merely for the sweat of the workout, but to be more thoroughly cleansed.

Turn my eyes from watching what is worthless;

give me life in your ways. (Psalm 119:37, BCP)

There is a German word that is applied to the odd pleasure, delight even, that one feels at the misfortune of others. *Schadenfreude* is a word composed of joining two words—damage/hurt and joy. Judging from the glee on the faces of the "live studio audience" and their unrestrained laughter, it would be safe to say that the producers of such television programs as *Dr. Phil*, *Steve Harvey*, *Marriage Boot Camp*, *Ex-Isle*, and *Keeping Up with the Kardashians* are all mining from the same vein of gold in the *schadenfreude* mine. If the word *schadenfreude* represents the pleasure one feels from another's hurt or disgrace, it could also extend to the delight one might feel in witnessing someone's experience of being publicly shamed. More simply, *schadenfreude* could just as easily contain *shame-joy* as it is does hurt-joy.

It seems that the networks, cable television, radio, and certainly the internet have each discovered a willing audience in those who, like Ham, choose not to uphold the dignity of their fellow human being, but rather to point out the flaw of the one who is fallen. Now, to be sure, I speak of Ham's trespass here as the telling of what he saw to his brothers when he could have chosen to just let his father sleep off his drunkenness in the privacy of his own tent. It's not entirely clear what Ham did that incurs the wrathful curse of his father—was it seeing his nakedness itself, or was it that he chose to announce what he saw to his kin (who then took action, without Ham's assistance, to protect their father from more public view)? It may be that biblical scholars have written Ph.D. dissertations that investigate the exact moment of Ham's offense. What we can probably all agree on is the strong intuitive parallel between whatever transgression takes place at Noah's tent flap and the violation of human dignity we see in our culture's exploitation of the nakedness of others. There are places and scenes that we who have promised "to uphold the dignity of every human being" are simply forbidden to witness, let alone seek out and take pleasure in.

Complicity

It should be clear that I am not talking about covering up misconduct or crimes in order that those who exploit the vulnerability of others may be protected. The recent film *Spotlight* chronicles the relentless efforts of a team of reporters at the *Boston Globe* that led to the exposure of crimes committed not only by hundreds of parish priests who engaged in pedophilia, but also by the extensive and systematic complicity of the Roman Church's hierarchy to hide the sins within its pastoral ranks. What distinguishes the movie *Spotlight* from being just a routine account of how journalism works is its choice to uncover the complicity of all involved, including the seasoned, hard-boiled editors who, we discover, had knowledge that there was something rotten in the system years before the story fully broke open.

What we see in this film is the opposite of reality television or radio, where those who suffer shame are publicly exposed so that the viewer can feel morally or emotionally more sanguine about themselves and their own predicament. Instead, *Spotlight* successfully unmasks how we all can succumb to tempting forces that would have us remain silent about cruelty or injustice or abuse rather than experience the discomfort of taking action to reveal the crime—afraid we will somehow make the victim, or ourselves, even more vulnerable, and amplifying the damage done them (and us).

I walked out of the movie theater's showing of *Spotlight* feeling as though the "spotlight" was on me and all the institutions with which

I've been affiliated: schools, churches, colleges, seminaries, all of which seek, almost by instinct, to protect themselves from outside scrutiny. I knew a lot of the people in the small theater where the film was shown. There were Roman Catholics, Jews, Episcopalians, agnostics, Unitarians, and those who were stridently anti-organized religion of any kind. I would venture to say that we all left the theater as though exposed, if not by a team of investigative journalists, then by our own consciences. As a result, though we were shaken, indignant, or tearful, we were further along in the work of upholding the dignity of all.

I mention the example of the investigative reporting portrayed in *Spotlight* in order to emphasize the difference between, on the one hand, the healthy and necessary disclosure of human sin for the advancement of justice, mercy, and healing, and on the other hand, the shaming of others for our own narcissistic elevation. By investigating what is at stake in Ham's discovery of his father's nakedness, and by guessing what his motives might be for reporting Noah's vulnerability to his brothers—and it is a guess here—I mean to make a parallel to the unrestrained and escalating delight with which our society seems to participate in the suffering of others.

Members of the Church are not immune to society's engagement in the shame-joy that falls within the linguistic field of *schadenfreude*. One has only to put up a barometer for it during a Sunday morning coffee hour. I confess my own indulgence. I cannot count the number of times when, as a parish priest, parishioners from a church in another denomination visit a Sunday morning worship service and then make it a point to say how troubled they are with their home parish because of some perceived "flaw" in the pastor. "She always preaches about the plight of blacks or gays or the poor." Or, "He and his wife are going through a divorce, and she's so wonderful, we just can't stay there." Or,

"That congregation is arguing about a new outreach to homeless families; it's just calmer to come to this church."

At first, the exposure of vulnerability in the neighboring parish might spark in us, especially if we are anxious and insecure about the value and worth of our own ministry, the feeling of a kind of satisfaction or uplift. "Well, for whatever inadequacies we might have here as Christ Church, at least we're not going through whatever is happening down the street at First Church of Christ." And a feeling of satisfaction, however shallow and fleeting, might tempt us with the fiction of superiority and invulnerability that says no one is leaving your congregation, even on that same Sunday morning, dissatisfied that your congregation just oozes with arrogance or that the preaching is utterly disconnected to the struggles that burden the people.

Gossip

Ham, the son of Noah, lurks within and among us, eager to point out the nakedness, the supposed flaws and foibles of our neighbor, even our relatives in the faith. There could be much worse things than to hear his story on a Sunday morning before coffee hour. Perhaps at that hour, more than at any other time in the week, do good, religious people engage in conversations that expose others for the sake of making ourselves feel better about our precarious place in the social order. Gossip is the name for that kind of talk, a word whose etymology brings us back to Ham.

Gossip is information that one feels free to share with a sibling, either in blood or in God. Generally, one doesn't share sensitive information about another with a perfect stranger, but with one who is considered a trusted friend or a kin. Ham speaks of his father's nakedness to his brothers outside his father's tent, arguably the first instance of true gossip in the Bible. I know that when I've shared gossip, yes, in the House of Bishops, it's with the understanding that these are my trusted brothers and sisters in God, with my "God-siblings." Whatever I've said about the strains and struggles and ineffective, bewildering decisions of a colleague, it's close to, if not the same as, what Ham uttered to his brothers outside his father's tent. As a result of that talk, things did not go well for his family. It's a chastening story, again, perhaps worth sharing on a Sunday morning, that could lead us to deeper reverence for those God has placed closest to us.

The Body of Christ

> . . . and those members of the body that we think less honorable we clothe with greater honor, and our less respectable members are treated with greater respect; whereas our more respectable members do not need this. But God has so arranged the body, giving the greater honor to the inferior member, that there may be no dissension within the body, but the members may have the same care for one another. (1 Corinthians 12:23–25)

One of Paul's greatest gifts to us is this profound understanding of the ordering of the Church as the Body of Christ. For so many of us, the body is not a source of honor or dignity, but of shame and vulnerability. We are pummeled with images of supposed bodily perfection in supermodels or movie stars. Pharmaceutical advertisements tell us how we can treat natural imperfections so that we don't have to feel self-conscious when we are getting our exercise at the gym or when we might be wearing short sleeves in public. Paul's pervasive use of the

Body to describe the intimate, unassailable connection of the Risen Christ with our maculate (that is, our blemished and stained) and mortal bodies invites us to transform our understanding of our own bodies and those of others.

It could be that the Church's obsession with matters of human sexuality is in some way an extended participation in the sin of Ham. To uphold one another's dignity is to honor a boundary and a border of another and to choose not to probe what demands to be treated "with greater honor," as Paul commends.

Years ago a friend described the crisis in her family when her brother disclosed that he was homosexual. My friend's parents considered themselves upstanding and prominent members of a church that was of a more conservative leaning, not likely to support the ordination of openly gay or lesbian candidates for the priesthood or the episcopate. The father was particularly shaken by the announcement of his son's sexual orientation, and even wondered aloud to my friend how he could still accept his son in his house or be seen with him in church. He even wondered if his son's being gay would somehow compromise his place of respect on the vestry and in the parish at-large. My friend was distressed at her father's feeling of shame, and wondered if there was something else going on in her dad's psyche that needed to be healed or freed. Why would his son's sexuality have such a contaminating effect?

As the holidays of Thanksgiving and Christmas approached, it was clear that his anxiety was waxing, and Deborah decided to confront her father. "Dad, I know you're struggling about Bill's news. What do you think is causing you so much suffering? Bill's the same. He's still your son. Nothing's really changed. What is it?" The father admitted that at first he wondered what people would think about his parenting and about the health of the family. But then he realized that he was not the only parent of a gay man in the church, and definitely not the only one in the town.

"It's not my standing in the church. None of that matters anyway."

"Then what's causing all the stress?"

"I'm ashamed to say it, but it's when I imagine Bill and his partner together having relations, my stomach just turns and my skin crawls!"

Without a pause and in a moment of inspiration, Deborah replied, "Well, Dad, to be honest, I feel the same way when I think of you and Mom having, as you say, relations."

And, something like scales fell from his eyes. They laughed. Indulging in what might be only described as justifiable—perhaps even holy—gossip, they began to name others in the church: the septuagenarian church organist and her husband, the prim matronly altar guide director and the friend with whom she had a "Boston marriage"[4] and who bore an uncanny resemblance in voice and physique to Sydney Greenstreet. Soon, they both realized that there are places no one but God is invited into, and that's how God has ordered things for the healthy functioning of the whole body, our own body, the body of society, and the Body of Christ, the Church.

Questions for Reflection and Discussion

- How does the story of "Noah's nakedness" relate to this age of social media? Are there risks of our becoming guilty of the trespass of Ham?

---

4. A term used in New England in the decades spanning the late nineteenth and early twentieth centuries to describe two women living together, independent of financial support from a man.

- When have you experienced the feeling of *schadenfreude,* pain-joy, or felt a certain satisfaction at someone else's suffering or shame? Have you known your local congregation or community to relish in that particular emotion? How was it expressed?
- Our baptismal vows contain the promise that we will uphold the dignity of every human being. How has the Church protected, or failed to protect, those whose stories or physical circumstances make them vulnerable to exposure like Noah's? How are the elderly treated in your family or local community?

3

Sarah's Laugh

Now Sarai, Abram's wife, bore him no children. She had an Egyptian slave-girl whose name was Hagar, and Sarai said to Abram, "You see that the LORD has prevented me from bearing children; go in to my slave-girl; it may be that I shall obtain children by her." And Abram listened to the voice of Sarai.

—Genesis 16:1–2

Let's sit with Sarah for a while. It will not be a comfortable visit. Let's stay with her and learn her story. It's the story of so many women in the world. It's a story so full of agony that we tend to read it with haste and pay more attention to her husband, Abraham. He always comes across as a hero of the Bible, the father of multitudes, the seed-bearer of faith. It's usually Abraham, not Sarah, who appears in our church's stained glass windows, his eyes looking up. But though the Bible relegates her to a supporting role, we need to hear Sarah's story as we examine the burden of shame and its power to distort the image of God we all bear.

Sarah has the most famous laugh in the Bible; do we remember any others? But hers is a laugh that hides more pain than it expresses hilarity. Her laugh emerges from a place of deep degradation. It's not a laugh of joy, but a laugh that reflects a self-understanding that is fraught with shame.[5] Her degradation is not explicitly mentioned in this scene when read, as it is in our church services, in isolation from everything that precedes the visit at Mamre. For what reason does Sarah have to be ashamed? Well, the norms of her time would tell her she has plenty. She suffers from the shame of infertility in a culture that depends on birth, and in the context of a promise from God to bless her family through her ability to produce offspring. Sarah is the "in-spite-of"—God tells her she will bear countless in spite of her being barren, in spite of her advanced age. Our own "more enlightened" society still places the burden of fertility on women. For some, being pregnant continues to be a sign of providential privilege, even in those who may otherwise disavow faith and religion. Shame and stigma can unjustly and cruelly attach to women who cannot bear children.

Exploitation

And there may be an additional source of her shame, besides that of her being infertile. In addition to feeling the shame of barrenness, Sarah may also be ashamed at having been exploited by her husband with Pharaoh for the sake of accruing family wealth. Abraham makes a deal with Pharaoh, giving his own wife over as sexual chattel while passing

---

5. See Genesis 18:1–15.

her off as his sister, so as to avoid the appearance of adultery. For her part, Sarah has no agency—no capacity, power, or freedom—to resist being used in this way. At the expense of her dignity, Abraham profits abundantly:

> And the woman was taken into Pharaoh's house. And for her sake he dealt well with Abram; and he had sheep, oxen, male donkeys, male and female slaves, female donkeys, and camels. (Genesis 12:15–16)

In this way Sarai-Sarah is quite possibly the first woman recorded in Scripture to be the victim of human trafficking. And it's not an isolated cruelty that happens only once to Sarah. Abraham repeats his exploitation later on when he "gives" his spouse to Abimelech (see Genesis 20). Abraham benefits enormously at Sarah's expense. Sarah pays the price of being forced into a relationship with a man outside of her marriage, of being exploited as property, and of suffering the shame that society attaches to the behavior of women. However, the Bible does not record any overt expression of her shame. Why would it? If the story is the account of the establishment of Abram's legitimacy as the father of the faith, why register the emotional, physical, and spiritual cost to Sarah of his deceptive dealings? Emphasizing the cost would undercut the narrative of success.

The cost to Sarah is the burden of shame. Though Sarah is not given voice in the scriptural record to express this burden, we might hear the voices of contemporary women who have been trafficked. Through their witness, Sarah's character can be appreciated in much more justice. Thanks in large part to the Rev. Becca Stevens of the Magdalene program and Thistle Farms,[6] a cooperative ministry that

---

6. http://thistlefarms.org/pages/our-mission

has empowered women who have been caught in lives of prostitution and human trafficking here in the United States, the Church is becoming much more aware of the damage such exploitation inflicts on a person. Here are statements of modern-day "Sarahs"—women who have been forced to sacrifice their bodies for either the gratification or the enrichment of others:

> "No matter what chains are broken, slavery is a condition of the heart."[7]

> "I cannot fail these girls by diverting my eyes from the invisible residue of slavery that clings to them like a shadow."[8]

> "Don't look at a homeless person and think she's just a bad person. Wonder what happened to her. Somebody damaged her at some point in her life to where she's out there and doesn't think she deserves any better."[9]

I suspect that sense of being unworthy of anything better—of slavery clinging to her like a shadow—is awakened in Sarah when her husband so eagerly greets the mysterious three visitors with one of his best calves. How did he acquire his prime herd of livestock? In Egypt, through his dealings with Pharaoh, the price paid by Sarah. Yet, these riches are offered up so easily by Abraham. Just as he offered her up. And still she is required to offer additional hospitality to the

---

7. Marquita Burke-DeJesus, *Radically Ordinary* (Mustang, OK: Tate Publishing, 2014), 159.
8. Ibid., 96.
9. Jennifer Clinger, Magdalene graduate, quoted in *Thrive!,* magazine of the Diocese of Chicago, Fall 2015.

strangers—to prepare the cake to accompany the meat on the table. Does she have a choice? Shame heaped on shame.

Transference

After their time in Egypt, Sarah and Abraham live all too aware of the promise God makes to Abraham that he will become the father of multitudes and the progenitor of nations. But how? We can imagine how Abraham and Sarah regarded each other—night after night, year after year, decade after decade—with each passing day a reminder of her barrenness. If her womb is the only means by which God's promise is to be accomplished, perhaps her infertility, her own body, becomes for them a sign not merely of failure, but even a threat to God's own purpose, an assault on the covenant? To Sarah, the promise of God must feel like a trap, a snare, something from which she cannot escape. Her shame must feel suffocating, airless, inescapable; trapped in her own body.

A possible escape occurs to her in her own maid-servant, Hagar. "It may be that I shall obtain children by her," she strategizes. In offering Hagar to Abraham, Sarah hopes for release from the trap, but she seeks this release through the exploitation of another woman, to whom she repeats the trauma done to her. Exploits her. Traffics her. Then shames her. Out of her own shame, Sarah transfers onto Hagar. As Simone Weil has written: "A hurtful act is the transference to others of the degradation which we bear in ourselves."[10]

---

10. Simone Weil, *Gravity and Grace* (New York: Taylor & Francis e-Library, 2003), 72.

It is in this inescapable whirlwind of shame, alone in the airless tent in the heat of the day, that she overhears the words of one of the visitors. She laughs to herself. A laugh of joy? Or a laugh of self-disdain? And how did the visitor hear her anyway? Is it the laugh of futility in the face of yet another assault on her person, yet more subjugation—this time by three men who have come to have their way with her? Or could this laugh be an indication that she senses the infiltration of love, invading her space, in order to give her back the dignity that had been deprived her?

Trauma and Suffering

At this point it must be acknowledged that women who have suffered infertility may not, understandably, take solace in the divine inter-vention that results in the births of Isaac (or of Samuel or John the Baptist—also born to barren women, as told later in Scripture). It seems that the only way Sarah's dignity can be restored, the only way she can count herself as blessed and not cursed, is through a miraculous birth. To the countless women who have suffered the actual pain of not being able to conceive or bring a child to term, Sarah is another one whose story can bruise them into a sense of inadequacy. Sarah can have a child at ninety, but not me? And it may not alleviate things to read the rest of the story. For Sarah, becoming a mother does not magically or auto-matically bring a life of pure joy. We can only imagine the suffering she herself must have endured when Abraham left with *her* only son up the mountain when demanded by God to sacrifice Isaac (Genesis 22).

This is the woman hidden behind the tent flap in the heat of the day. When her husband rushes out to meet the mysterious strangers, we could almost imagine her trepidation. Will the arrival of these visitors be yet another occasion for her to be exploited? How much does she have left to give? It's likely that behind the famous laugh is a cynical hardness, wariness with a life that has seemed like nothing but a series of repeated trauma.

Individuals who have experienced violence and trauma in the past are more vulnerable to future exploitation, as the psychological effect of trauma is often long lasting and challenging to overcome. Traffickers, who recognize the vulnerabilities left by these prior abuses, may target victims of domestic violence, sexual assault, war and conflict, or social discrimination. Violence and abuse may be normalized, or beliefs of shame or unworthiness may lead to future susceptibility to human trafficking.[11]

The encounter under the shade could be read as God's redress of the wrongs inflicted on Sarah, as a break in the long cycle of indignities that has been her story up to this point. Firmly convinced that she deserves nothing, the visitors disrupt everything she knows about what is possible:

> They said to him, "Where is your wife Sarah?" And he said, "There, in the tent." Then one said, "I will surely return to you in due season, and your wife Sarah shall have a son." And Sarah was listening at the tent entrance behind him. Now Abraham and Sarah were old, advanced in age; it had ceased to be with Sarah after the manner of women. So Sarah laughed to herself, saying, "After I have grown old, and my husband is old, shall I have pleasure?" The LORD said to Abraham, "Why did Sarah laugh, and say, 'Shall I

---

11. National Human Trafficking Resource Center, https://traffickingresource center.org/what-human-trafficking/human-trafficking/victims

indeed bear a child, now that I am old?' Is anything too wonderful
for the LORD? At the set time I will return to you, in due season,
and Sarah shall have a son." (Genesis 18:9–14)

The Three Visitors

Christians have, from early on, interpreted the arrival of the three visitors as a social call from God the Holy Trinity itself. Though there is
nothing in the Hebrew Bible that mentions the Trinity, this has not
prevented early Christian readers from understanding the story as an
account of the blessings that accrue to those who share hospitality with
strangers. The writer of the New Testament's Letter to the Hebrews
makes a direct reference to Genesis 18 when urging readers, "Do not
neglect to show hospitality to strangers, for by that some have enter-
tained angels without knowing it" (Hebrews 13:2).

Though Sarah's story may not bring much comfort to those who
feel stigmatized, the encounter with the visitors under the oaks of
Mamre may offer a sign of God's desire to heal the damaging effects of
shame. Countless Christians have prayed with the icon variously called
"Old Testament Hospitality" or "The Holy Trinity," with the most
famous rendering made by the fourteenth-century Russian artist and
iconographer Andrei Rublev. In it the terebinths are represented in the
background by a thin tree. The dwelling place of Abraham and Sarah
looks more like the architecture of a Dr. Seuss book than a Middle
Eastern tent. These odd details in an icon can lead us to consider that
this is a depiction of truths that are deeper, eternally occurring, even
surreal (that is, super-real), greater than what we might expect from a
more direct representation of an event with a beginning, middle, and
end at a remote time in the past.

The three figures have wings, signaling that they are transcendent beings. Again, we are regarding truths that have a reality beyond what we normally encounter. Although the icon presents them as other-worldly, they still need to eat. At the center of the table where they are seated is a dish of some kind, a bowl containing food. We can infer from the passage in Genesis that it's either the meat that Abraham's servant has prepared or one of Sarah's cakes. Those who have shared the Eucharistic feast frequently will feel drawn to inferring a connection between that table and an altar where the Christ's Body and Blood is offered.

Many elements of the icon are worth contemplation, but what might be most relevant is the quality of the regard of the three visitors. Having spent many years sitting and praying with reproductions of Rublev's icon, I have experienced a strange thing. At first, the eyes of the Beings seem to be directed at each other. As scholars have described it to me, the figure on the left is meant to be the First Person of the Trinity, the Father, with the Son at the center and the Holy Spirit on the right. The gaze of Christ and the Holy Spirit seems at first to be directed toward the Creator, but, over time, I have experienced the eyes of all three looking out from the surface of the painting and directed toward the viewer—me! I would be reluctant to admit to being the object of the Holy Trinity's attention, but over the years I have heard many others sharing the same experience.

Restoration

The gaze is penetrating and yet gentle. The eyes of the Holy Three seem to look into places of my soul and being that would otherwise not be open to being disclosed. Though their scrutiny may judge and see those places within me that are distorted and damaged by sin, their gazes do not condemn. Their eyes reflect a special kind of knowing that allows me to look into myself in the spirit of love. Under their penetrating survey, I feel the grip of shame loosen.

Though Sarah is hidden in the tent and has had no conversation with the three visitors, they seem to know her nonetheless. After their meal, one announces that she will be with child when he returns. Knowing what we know of Sarah's plight and concealed burden, a burden she bears alone, it is not unreasonable to imagine that what causes her laughter is not only the outlandish prediction of a child, but the surprise, perhaps even the relief, in suddenly having her pain recognized by another. Though concealed behind the door of the tent, within the confining pain of shame, the prediction of a child reveals a knowledge on the part of the stranger that is both penetrating and encompassing. She is seen, fully recognized, and utterly known for who she is. To be known, through and through, and not rejected or condemned, marks the beginning of healing.

It is the same with us. Every time we open the service of the Holy Eucharist with the prayer called the Collect for Purity, we can imagine ourselves, open and accepted, by the same visitors who appear outside Sarah's tent. Each of those visitors invokes the words we so often pray, thus placing ourselves within the scene around the divine table of hospitality:

Almighty God, to you all hearts are open, all desires known, and from you no secrets are hid: Cleanse the thoughts of our hearts by the inspiration of your Holy Spirit, that we may perfectly love you, and worthily magnify your holy Name; through Christ our Lord. (BCP, 355)

Spiritual Friendship

One of the most powerful experiences I have had in church was in a small group of men who met around a low round table in the old rectory. Though the old New England townhouse had been converted into offices, like so many in our churches, it still had the feel of a home. It's hard to shake the sense that the rooms in this building used to be the dwelling place of clergy families in decades past. Even as I sat at my desk and worked on the computer or the telephone, I would often stare off into what was once a dining room, kitchen, or family room—I had a strange compulsion to move my office-study with some unsettling frequency—and imagine the voices and the conversations that the walls of each room had heard over the past century. I always had the sense that conversation among members of the clergy families that once lived in the house, and then later, the vestry meetings, youth groups, or the myriad committee meetings that took place in the old rectory, were still going on, as eternal as the conversation that is depicted in the icon of the Holy Trinity.

One year, I felt myself going through a period of some spiritual funk. It seemed that life in the church where I served had become fruitless. All the outward indicators of parish health seemed to point to a relatively healthy congregation. The touted average Sunday attendance was not rising by leaps and bounds, but it was holding steady with some incremental growth. Income from pledges was strong. The youth group had effective leadership. The parish had a reputation for bold outreach and advocacy for matters of justice and peace, both locally and abroad. The place was a beehive of activity.

But I felt an inner disconnection. Despite the encouraging compliments of my bishop, and of the wardens and vestry of the parish, I felt incapable of feeling the joy of the gospel. Something was missing. Having experienced and been treated for depression for some time, I was certain that the lack I was experiencing was something quite different. In my visits with others in the parish, I realized that I was not alone. Others were in a similar place, a wilderness, but we were suffering "alone together," unwilling to reveal just how hollow it seemed to be, abandoned by God. As a priest, I felt a sense of shame in my inner lack of enthusiasm; that is, of fullness of spirit. Mixed with that shame was fear of being found out as a fraud.

Then one day as I was preparing for a weekday celebration of the Eucharist in January, I came upon a passage from the writings of Aelred of Rievaulx, a twelfth-century Cistercian abbot who is most famous for his treatise *On Spiritual Friendship*.

> But what happiness, what security what joy to have someone to whom you dare to speak on terms of equality as to another self; one to whom you need have no ear to confess your failings; one to whom you can unblushingly make know what progress you have made in the spiritual life; one to whom you can entrust all the secrets of your heart and before whom you can place all your plans! What, therefore, is more pleasant than so to unite to oneself the spirit of another and of two to form one, that no boasting is thereafter to be feared, no suspicion to be dreaded, no correction of one by the other to cause pain, no praise on the part of one to bring a charge of adulation from the other. "A friend," says the Wise Man, "is the medicine of life." [Sirach 6:16] Excellent, indeed, is that saying. For medicine is not more powerful or more efficacious for our wounds in all our temporal needs than the possession of a friend who meets every misfortune joyfully, so that, as the Apostle says,

shoulder to shoulder, they bear one another's burdens. [Galatians 6:2] . . . And, a thing even more excellent than all these considerations, friendship is a stage bordering upon that perfection which consists in the love and knowledge of God, so that man from being a friend of his fellow man becomes a friend of God, according to the word of the Savior in the Gospel: "I will not now call you servants, but my friends" [John 15:15].[12]

There is a curious word Christians have to describe the feeling that overcomes one and says, "That's it! That's what I've been missing all along." Or when one suddenly sees within oneself the need to turn from a path one was committed to but has suddenly seemed to have led to a place far from God's promises. I was *convicted*—abruptly aware that my practice as a priest in this parish was more akin to being the activities director on a cruise liner rather than one who sought, pointed toward, and nourished such friendship as Aelred so eloquently extolled.

The Pastorates

Yes, I had, and have, a deep and trusted best friend in my wife, now of over twenty-five years, with whom I have made a home and a family of three remarkable children. Yes, I had, and have, cherished relationships among former college and seminary classmates. And yes, I had trusted relationships among clergy colleagues with whom I could let down the persona, the mask, of being the competent parish priest. And I had a trusting friend outside the Church, a prominent businessman and

---

12. Aelred, *Spiritual Friendship*, II, 11–14; English translation by Mary Eugenia Laker, SSND (Spencer, MA, 1977), 72–73.

civic leader in the region with whom I rowed every Friday morning. These relationships, primarily outside the congregation and even the religious field of the Church, were and are bedrock for me, essential to my health, well-being, indeed my life.

But after reading Aelred's *Spiritual Friendship,* it starkly dawned on me that there was a gulf between the friendship that is exhibited in the icon of the Holy Trinity and the normative practice among members of the congregation. We were known by many in the town and in the diocese as being a very "activist" parish, but did we know—really know—the "stage bordering on that perfection which consists in the love and knowledge of God" in our friendship with one another and with our neighbor. I could not see it. And if those occasions of sharing and deepening friendship were there, I was too busy serving as the cruise director on the ship of the parish that I couldn't share in those occasions myself. Though I may have been the chief celebrant at the services of Holy Communion—that is, the Holy Sharing—I myself was still hungry for the friendship that Jesus himself enjoyed among those he served.

My discovery of Aelred led me to invite a small group to reflect on the health of our relationships in the parish. We did not need to examine a conflict or a state of contentiousness. We had natural and healthy "conversations" among us, some of them quite passionate, ranging from our support of the Palestinian people, to marriage equality, to our care of creation and climate justice. What some of us were missing was simply time to pray, to sit together in each other's presence, to reflect, and to experience God's love in silence and in contemplative conversation in God's Word.

So, we tried several things. Some worked, and some did not. We encouraged members of the parish to gather in homes for what we called "pastorates," small neighborhood groups akin to the foyer or Coventry groups that formed after the destruction of Coventry Cathedral during the Battle of Britain in World War II. Having looked at a map of the region served by the church, we designated conveners to invite neighbors, those who lived within a few miles of their house.

People would gather, sit in silence in a living or family room, and perhaps read a passage designated to be read at the Sunday worship. People were encouraged to speak what was the moment of highest energy they found in the passage. They might share the one word or phrase from the passage that struck them as the most comforting or distressing or confusing without explaining why. After five or ten minutes—at least five minutes—of silence, a more wide-ranging discussion of the Bible passage followed. More silence followed, with the participants just sitting with eyes closed, or sitting with eyes gazing at each other's eyes—just like the Rublev icon. Then people were invited to pray, by name or in silence, for those in the room, and for those in the parish, in the community, and in the world.

I felt the pastorates had infinite promise for the renewal and strengthening of our parish, but they had only limited success. The one or two groups that really took off—and I hope they're still going strong—were established by leaders who were wonderfully persistent in their invitations. They kept at it, keeping lists of parishioners who had moved into their neighborhood, making phone calls to enlist prayer and assistance when one of our brothers or sisters had a personal struggle that they were sufficiently comfortable sharing, and inviting me as the priest to come every few months to offer a home communion.

Perhaps the power of the "pastorate" consisted in the homeyness of the experience. When we open our home, we open up a space that may not be completely polished or perfect. Our mantles and end tables may not pass the "white-glove" test of cleanliness. Photographs of our imperfect family gatherings are on display, and we may show ourselves for whom we truly are. Sarah and Abraham, far from perfect in so many ways that we, or their own society, may have been, are still the hosts of none other than God, the Holy Trinity. And Sarah and Abraham are accepted for who they are, drawn into God's mission in a way that is, well, laughable. That was what we boldly attempted to accomplish in the pastorates.

The Aelred Group

We also attempted something called the Aelred Group. This was very similar in format and structure to the pastorates, but it was limited to men. The idea was that apart from a very long-running (twenty-plus years) gathering of men who were mostly retired and met early every Friday morning for coffee and bagels, we did not have an occasion for men to sit in silence, pray, read Scripture, and share the burdens and joys of their hearts. Our society is one that encourages, if not enforces, a spirit of competition and distrust among men. As a result, we often feel we cannot trust each other, sometimes behaving more like neighborhood dogs that need to mark each other's territory. The buffer zones among us so contradict the image of being One in the Body of Christ that we more often feel like adversaries or opponents rather than brothers.

Every Thursday night, about five or six of us gathered around a table in the old rectory. We read a passage from Aelred himself, offered a prayer, and then asked each other if, and where, we had seen Jesus in the past week. After a few weeks, we could feel a level of trust infuse the group; some of us felt free to say that we seemed to have missed seeing Jesus, or that we had forgotten to look, or that our faith was faltering. One of our members, a retired executive who had left work in the corporate world to stay home to raise children, became like an abbot of the group. The younger of us, caught up with the addiction to accomplish and advance in career and status, myself included, were usually reminded by Pete what was really essential in life. As the fox in St. Exupery's *The Little Prince* would say, "What is essential is invisible to the eye."

After Pete was diagnosed with cancer, we continued to sit with him, both on the Aelred nights and then at his home as he entered hospice. It was not long after that the rest of us, succumbing to the demands of our calendars of accomplishment and achievement, decided to disband the group. I sometimes mourn it still, now over ten years since its dissolution, though the bonds that were formed around that table endure and give me comfort to this day. I wonder if perhaps such trust and spiritual intimacy among men is just too intense to be sustained in our contemporary society.

It wouldn't be surprising if the suggestion of forming such a gathering as the Aelred Group in many of our staid congregations would be met with the same dismissive laugh that Sarah shared with herself behind the tent flap. That laugh won't prevent God from enlisting us into God's mission, however complicated, disrupting, unjust, and unwelcome that mission may seem to us.

Questions for Reflection and Discussion

- Sarah's laugh may indicate her sense of unworthiness and shame, a way of laughing off the promise of a new chapter in her life. When a surprising good thing comes your way (a compliment, a gift, a happy turn of events), how do you usually respond? Do you trust it? If not, why not?

- Is it easy or hard for you to receive the attention of others?
- Reproductions of the icon by Andrei Rublev mentioned in this chapter are widely available. What would it be like for trusted friends or companions to sit for a time in silence in a similar arrangement within each other's gaze? How uncomfortable would it make you? Would it become more comfortable over time with practice? Could it be healing to the lingering sense of shame?

4

Create in Me a Clean Heart

David sent someone to inquire about the woman. It was reported,
"This is Bathsheba daughter of Eliam, the wife of Uriah the Hittite."
So David sent messengers to get her, and she came to him, and he lay
with her. . . . When the wife of Uriah heard that her husband was
dead, she made lamentation for him. When the mourning was over,
David sent and brought her into his house, and she became his wife,
and bore him a son.

—2 Samuel 11:3–4a, 26–27

Sitting before a Congressional hearing investigating the fixing of prices for Daraprim, a medicine used to halt parasitic infections in people with compromised immune systems, such as those with HIV, a young man faces stern questions from his fellow citizens. The congressman asks him if he has any remorse for his role in raising

the price of Daraprim by five thousand percent, putting it out of the
reach of those who need it most.[13] The investigators share stories of a
single mother, afflicted with the AIDS virus, who struggles to make
ends meet to raise her children on income she ekes out with tips as
a waitress. The congressman asks the young man, "Does it matter to
you that your pricing of this drug has essentially cut off this young
woman from her lifeline?"

The videoed testimony is excruciating to watch. The young man,
Martin Shkreli, is dressed casually for this appearance before mil-
lions who will have access to the hearing. As he prepares to respond
to the questions of the panel, a smirk appears over his face. "On the
advice of counsel, I invoke my Fifth Amendment privilege against self-
incrimination and respectfully decline to answer your question."

More damning evidence is offered. A member of the House panel
suggests to him that there are questions that would not lead to self-
incrimination and asks if he will make any response or statement. "I
choose to listen to the advice of my counsel, not yours."

As the hearing continues, Shkreli adopts an even more cavalier
demeanor, looking away, as though distracted. As a congressman begs
him to use whatever influence he still has with his pharmaceutical company to make more accessible the needed drug by lowering its price, he
returns an expression of utter disdain and bemusement, crossing one
leg over the other and leaning back in his chair.

---

13. Carolyn Johnson, "Pharma Bro Shkreli stays silent before Congress, calls law-
makers imbeciles in Tweet," *Washington Post,* February 4, 2016.

Shamelessness

Though his pricing practices represent, in the words of one panel member, all that is wrong with Pharma, the collective name given to the pharmaceutical manufacturers, marketers, and distributors, Shkreli clearly demonstrates no remorse. The stories of the suffering caused by his company's profit gouging of Daraprim has no influence on him. He displays no compassion, no inner reflection, no relationship to his customers. He appears utterly impenetrable—one is tempted to say without soul. For many who witnessed Martin Shkreli's appearance before the House Committee on Oversight and Governmental Reform on Thursday, February 4, 2016, his complete lack of any sense of guilt or complicity in his company's practices invokes nothing short of extreme outrage and made him, as one commented, "the most hated human being in America."

Such harsh comments are not unusual on social media. The vocabulary for outrage has expanded as a result of the immediacy of the media—two words that clearly share the same etymological root. Online, there is no margin between the initial experience of a moral or aesthetic assault and the impulse to respond with indignation and horror, even hatred. To borrow Martin Buber's useful distinction, we fall prey to the temptation to drain a person of his or her sanctity as a child of God, however fallen, and to deny them their full personhood, treating them more as an object, an IT, than as one with whom we share Being in this world, a THOU. That temptation is exponentially stronger online than it may be "in the flesh."

But still, Martin Shkreli's alleged sins, if indeed true, and the obvious callousness he showed on his day in the U.S. Capitol were shining examples of an individual's habit to relate to his neighbor as merely a means to an end. In Shkreli's case the end is clearly self-enrichment, perhaps mixed with the intoxicating thrill of exerting power to influence market forces at his own whim. There appeared to be no capacity to feel compassion, empathy, or any connection with those whose lives were directly affected by his (alleged) unethical financial scheming. Had he felt such a connection, if the stories of the women and children whose suffering was drastically exacerbated by the exorbitant price hike of the needed drug were those of his own sister or children, might he have felt remorse? From his smirks and his post-hearing caustic tweet in which he referred to the members of the House panel as "imbeciles," even such compassion on his part would be hard to imagine. I suspect that it was the absence of remorse, the sheer *shamelessness* of his non-testimony, that led the commentators on social media to question not merely his sense of morality, but his humanity.

   This leads me to wonder if the phenomenon of shame could indeed have a positive function. If we saw Shkreli express sadness, remorse, or shame before the panel, even if we doubted its sincerity, observers may have not been so quick to question whether they had an actual human being before them. To put it another way, perhaps it is shame that can rescue a sinner from the power of sin to dehumanize a person, to so distort the image of God within one as to make their humanity seem unrecognizable.

Heinousness

Scripture offers many examples of people who have behaved like Martin Shkreli. We can think back to the first act of physical violence, the murder of Abel by his brother Cain. That hateful act was borne out of envy. Abel's offering was accepted by God. Cain's was not. The sense of not having God's favor was intolerable to Cain, and by killing Abel he commits the ultimate act of an I-It relationship. Abel is seen as dispensable in Cain's eyes. He murders in order to attain the end of gaining God's blessing. The obvious fault in Cain's reason is, of course, that God never seems to have withdrawn God's love or favor from him in the first place.

But the most obvious example of one who treats a neighbor with such murderous disregard is the story of David's rape of Bathsheba and his plot to kill her husband, Uriah, in order to cover up his guilt. The narrative of David's heinous gratification of his own desire at the expense of the dignity of Bathsheba and the life of Uriah represents one of the most troubling moments in the Bible. It's a story rarely read in the Sunday lectionary, and probably even less frequently shared in settings like Sunday school or confirmation class where we assume it would assault tender ears. If read in church, the story from 2 Samuel should probably come with the warning that precedes certain television shows: "This show contains scenes that some viewers may find disturbing," or "Viewer discretion advised."

It's striking that, as I mention David, the King of Israel, the exemplar of God's favor, I am putting his sinfulness in the same league as Martin Shkreli. In fact, on a scale of grotesqueness, David's sin is worse. And yet, David is exalted as the most important of all the kings of Israel. Jesus himself welcomes being hailed by his followers as the Son of David. His triumphal entry into Jerusalem with the earsplitting shout of "Hosanna! Son of David!" suggests that he sees his authority is at least partially derived from the authority of David.

What makes him so different from our Pharma friend is his remorse—the heartfelt and sincere sense of shame that cuts him to the core. The intensity of David's self-examination and his dramatic repentance is barely indicated from the short verse in the account of the story in 2 Samuel. The writer of this drama only gives one small verse to the pivoting of condemnation, shame, forgiveness, and absolution:

> David said to Nathan, "I have sinned against the LORD." Nathan said to David, "Now the LORD has put away your sin; you shall not die." (2 Samuel 12:13)

If we were to stop reading with this verse, we would have grounds to be deeply bothered. The sheer scale of David's sin warrants a much more fulsome confession and expression of self-loathing. Why does he not turn toward himself the hostility that he previously expressed toward the fictitious man whom Nathan had presented as having stolen the cherished lamb? His sense of righteous indignation at the rich man for having slaughtered a lamb was so ignited as to demand not merely that he restore the lamb to the poor man, but that he be condemned to death. After Nathan concludes this hypothetical case, David's reaction is intense:

> Then David's anger was quickly kindled against the man. He said to Nathan, "As the LORD lives, the man who has done this deserved to die; he shall restore the lamb fourfold, because he did this thing, and because he had no pity. (2 Samuel 12:5)

In comparison to the intense rage David feels against a privileged man who stole and callously slew a lamb, his sole statement "I have sinned against the LORD" seems utterly tepid and undeserving of any leniency on God's part. Indeed, it seems hard to fathom how quickly Nathan could declare that David's several offenses in this story—abuse of the privilege of power, rape, adultery, murder, and deceit—are to be absolved. If one were to weigh the king's offenses against those of the hypothetical rich man in Nathan's indicting parable, David would come out the guiltier, by far. How can he get off so easily?

That lack of proportionality is only one issue we might have with this whole disturbing story of royal accountability. We might be even more horrified by the fact that the story continues with the consequences of David's sin not being fully "put away," but rather transferred onto the child who is the result of David's assault of Bathsheba. As David demands when he is first told the parable of the stolen and slain lamb, someone must die. And as it happens, it is a newborn, one whose innocence bears some parallel relation with the lamb of the poor man in Nathan's parable.

Remorse

Scripture provides us with a window into the depths of David's remorse in the words of the fifty-first psalm. Arguably, Psalm 51 is a close second to Psalm 23 as the most recited in the long history of choral music and hymnody. Scriptural scholars have traditionally placed this psalm under the category of a lament, as it expresses deep sorrow and a plea for help or deliverance from the threat of an enemy. Psalm 51 is transmitted down through the ages with this inscription: "To the leader. A Psalm of David, when the prophet Nathan came to him, after he had gone in to Bathsheba." This subtitle invites us to read the psalm as an amplification of the disturbingly terse and tepid verse confession found in 2 Samuel: "I have sinned against the LORD."

Psalm 51 is an exploration, not only of guilt and remorse for having committed an egregious act, but of shame itself. The petitioner of this psalm (and let us here, for the sake of simplicity, suspend the hermeneutic of suspicion that may have good textual, critical, and historical reason to doubt the authorship of David) not only expresses regret, but the depth of his agony characterizes what we experience as shame. Why do I say this? Because nowhere does David speak of his actual sin. Apart from the inscription to the psalm, there is nothing the poet says that actually indicates what he has done wrong. Instead, he complains that wickedness is a constituent part of his being, as though in his body. The psalm thus rings true and echoes deeply with those through the ages who know something of shame. It is a bodily thing.

> Indeed, I have been wicked from my birth
> a sinner from my mother's womb. (Psalm 51:6, BCP, 656)

If guilt says, "I have done wrong and committed a sin," and shame says, "not only that, but I *am* wrong, and I *am* a sin," Psalm 51 does not shy away from the more agonizing effects of feeling oneself cut off from God's presence. The translation from the New Revised Standard Version of the Bible suggests that there was never a time in the speaker's life when he was not under divine disfavor and judgment:

> Indeed, I was born guilty,
> a sinner when my mother conceived me. (Psalm 51:5)

I read this verse as an expression of the depths of shame rather than as a statement to support that problematic doctrine of Original Sin discussed when we examined the sin of Adam and Eve in the first chapter. The psalmist blurts out what so many of us experience when forced to reckon with a sin we have committed that has caused harm.

Awareness of having done something so egregious, so heinous, so outside of what we had considered our real self, so often leads us to feel that if we have done any good at all, it's in spite of our deepest, truest nature, which is broken, distorted, filthy, self-centered, vicious, slothful, and so on. Fill in the blank. The verse gives voice to the agony that stems from being separated from God. Where else in our public life but in worship are we invited into such a tender and raw place of self-awareness?

Salutary Shame

This brings us to ask some difficult questions: Might shame actually have a positive function? Is shame always damaging to the soul? Could it be possible that shame, like other negative emotions—anger, envy, sorrow—is part of the created order, part of what it means to be fully alive, fully human? Is there such a thing as salutary shame, shame that can lead us to healthy, more profound, and holy relationships with God and our neighbor?

It is hard to consider the spiritual, emotional, or social values of shame when we are in its grip. I know when I feel shame: it comes like a wave of fire over my scalp, landing in my gut where it might twist and burn. Shame is so unwelcome and can be so disabling that it is no wonder our culture, with Dr. Freud's permission, dismisses it as unnatural and destructive to the development of a healthy personality. But I find that remembering when I felt shame at a time sufficiently in the past that it no longer provokes its previous sting, then—with the gifts that come from reflecting at a safer distance—I can allow that shame has led me to some growth and enrichment of my relationships with God and neighbor.

So looking back, way back, I remember an event shortly after I was first ordained to the priesthood and serving in an urban parish that was host to the largest feeding ministry in the city. As is often the case, the parish itself could not absorb and support all the costs of running the soup kitchen, which fed breakfast and lunch to nearly two hundred people every day. The Community Soup Kitchen relied on the generosity of its neighbors to provide financial contributions to meet the budget, which grew year by year as national, state, and local safety nets for the mentally ill, the disabled, and the unemployed were shrinking in the late 1980s and early 90s. Times have not changed.

A large fundraising event was held where donors were invited to share a supper hosted at the Soup Kitchen itself, which was located in the church's large parish hall. Contributors included local neighbors as well as faculty and administrators of the city's large, prestigious university, which strove to foster happy "town-gown" relations. There were also many middle-class professionals who lived in the suburbs and who saw a healthy city as a good thing for their own neighborhoods.

With such a large and wide-ranging constituency, it would have been wise to assume that not everyone at the fundraiser was a member of the church that hosted the Community Soup Kitchen. Yes, it should have been obvious that not everyone there was even Christian. As the evening program got underway, there was a call to prayer before the meal. The rector, my new boss, asked me on the spur of the moment to offer the blessing. I cannot recall the words I uttered verbatim, I only remember doing the best I could to adapt the rhythms of the collects of the Book of Common Prayer, addressing the God of abundance, hospitality, generosity, and justice, thanking God for implanting in our hearts a vision of God's Realm in such a way as to inspire our establishment and support of the Community Soup Kitchen where all may know the friendship of Jesus our Savior. In whose name we prayed. Amen.

Well, there were a few "amens." Maybe. But what I remember so clearly is the angry objection of a prominent educator who wanted me to know, then and there, that he was utterly offended by my prayer because I had offered it in the name of Jesus. Didn't I know how many of the Jewish community were in attendance? Was I aware how many agnostics, atheists, and Muslims supported the important work of the Soup Kitchen, not because it was part of the Church's outreach, but in spite of it? He was himself a refugee from Nazi Germany who lost family members in the death camps in Poland. "When I see a cross," he said, "my first feeling is fear." And then he concluded, "To assume that all those who supported feeding the hungry were members of the same Christian faith is presumptuous and insensitive. Shame." The exact wording of my prayer doesn't come to me, but his rebuke has stuck with me, even a quarter of a century later. Especially that last word, delivered as he briskly walked away.

Now, this episode is not unusual. Probably every rookie deacon, priest, and bishop has inadvertently touched a rail that has led to an immediate reckoning of our ignorance and lack of awareness of those in the room who do not share our particular history, perspective, theology, or experience of privilege. It's a commonplace assumption that many who have entered the ordained ministry are generally kind people who appreciate the warmth of working together with a variety of people. To learn that something we've said, prayed, or preached has either caused or awakened latent pain can cause grief.

I have to admit that my own feelings ran a wide gamut in the aftermath of this man's sharp reproach. First, there was confusion. What was happening? At one moment I was praying, imagining we who were about to share a little portion of the Kingdom of God through our table fellowship on behalf of the hungry. The next moment, a man, his face flushed with anger, was telling me how much I had hurt him. At one moment, in the midst of his outburst, I may have felt a kind of floating away, as though I was separating from myself. What? Where were we? Am I here? Is this really happening? All I could manage to say was, "Oh. Oh, no. I'm so sorry." I'm not even sure the man heard me.

Rebuke and Repentance

Just to go back to Nathan's rebuke of David for a moment. How did David receive the new awareness that he had sinned? If one only reads the passage from 2 Samuel, one would have to surmise that it hardly registered at all. All he says is, "I have sinned." Textual experts of the Bible may have a perfect explanation for why David's statement of repentance is so terse—he doesn't even say, "Oh my God, I have really made a horrible mess and committed a grievous error." At least not according to the writer of the book of Samuel. Scriptural scholars will no doubt call this a stretch, my own reading *into the text* what is really not there, but I would suggest that the brevity of David's confession is a result of the enormity of his feeling of shame. He is simply too stunned by shame to get anything else out of his mouth.

As he repairs into his own chamber to ask for forgiveness and mercy upon the child who is born to Bathsheba, it is there, in that more burrowed and inward place, that he can pour out the agony of his shame. The fruit of that anguish is the great penitential psalm, Psalm 51, that we recite on our knees on Ash Wednesday. It also contains verses that are interspersed throughout the daily offices of the church:

> V. Create in us clean hearts, O God;
> R. And sustain us with your Holy Spirit. (BCP, 98, 122)

After reeling from the rebuke, I spent the next few days ricocheting between shame and anger. The dialogue went something like this:

Shame: Oh, God. I have reopened the wounds of the Holocaust in my neighbor. How can I have done such a thing? What was I thinking? Why wasn't I thinking? "I am a worm, and no man." (This could be an economically concise statement of shame from another psalm of lament, Psalm 22—the one Jesus himself quotes from the cross when he asks why God has abandoned him. For those who are wracked with shame, and who find themselves repeating this verse, it feels rather like a slight on worms rather than a "dissing" or a diminution of being human.)

Anger: Now hold on a second! What gives that guy the right to rebuke me for praying in my own house?! Doesn't he realize he was the guest of the church? If I were in his synagogue, would I have had the audacity to criticize the prayers of the rabbi? In a mosque, would I criticize the Imam? What gives here?

Shame: And yes, he was a guest. And you presumed he was like you, believed like you do. How was that hospitable? If you wanted to express and display the love of Jesus, you could have been more courteous, more aware and respectful of the sensibilities of your neighbors who, by the way, are helping, however indirectly, to pay for your livelihood as a priest.

Anger: Pshaw. You just don't want to acknowledge Jesus. Remember what he said, "Those who are *ashamed* of me and of my words, of them the Son of Man will be ashamed when he comes in his glory and the glory of the Father and of the holy angels" (Luke 9:26).

Shame: I don't know what to say. All I know is that the man was hurt, and the mention of Jesus brought up the whole tragic history of the Church's complicit silence in a time of unimaginable cruelty. That wasn't my intention, but there it is, and it pains me to acknowledge it.

Anger: Then why bother? You're not responsible for the sins of the world, are you? Do you believe you're that powerful? Wow.

Shame: No. But I am part of this human race. Part of a religion that bears guilt. I feel it, and it hurts. God help us.

Anger: Yeah. God help us get over it.

Shame: It's not that simple or easy.

And so it goes. A choice between, on the one hand, fully owning having caused a hurt in a soul, and on the other hand, dismissing the man's pain as being threatening to my own integrity as a Christian because I offered a prayer on "my own turf."

There are clearly plenty of nuances in this little episode, which I have to admit pales in comparison to the drama that took place on the rooftops in Jerusalem and the battlefield of Uriah the Hittite. I offer it from my memory precisely because it's the kind of event that probably occurs to us with much more regularity than the larger-scale moral lapses that are, I pray, much less frequent in our lives. Almost every day we are at risk of colliding with others by saying something that is presumptuous or that offends. Occasionally, we are called on it. And we are given a chance, thank God, to make a choice. Do we put up our shields of self-defense, choosing to listen to what our defensive anger has to tell us? In many instances this is indeed warranted, wise, and healthy. But I am beginning to wonder if, in all our therapeutic models, our support groups, and our clergy wellness sessions, we are too readily discarding the hard learning that might come if we at least allow shame to enter the conversation to teach us as well.

Questions for Reflection and Discussion

- This chapter explores the possibility that, in certain cases, shame plays a healthy role in leading us to the needed awareness of our relationship with and accountability toward others. What examples can you think of when shame has led to a more caring, just, and loving attitude toward someone else?
- Can you relate to the "dialogue" between Shame and Anger recounted in this chapter when the author is confronted for not being sufficiently aware of his audience?
- What happens to you, and within you, when you are confronted with an uncomfortable truth about your behavior or something you said that caused hurt?
- Who are the trusted "Nathans" in your life and ministry? Have you been called on to serve that role for someone else? Is there still shame, or has it been dispelled?

5

Yet More Wonderfully Restored

As he walked along, he saw a man blind from birth. His disciples asked him, "Rabbi, who sinned, this man or his parents, that he was born blind?" Jesus answered, "Neither this man nor his parents sinned; he was born blind so that God's works might be revealed in him. We must work the works of him who sent me while it is day; night is coming when no one can work. As long as I am in the world, I am the light of the world."

—John 9:1–5

Where do you feel shame? I do not mean to ask when in your life's timeline have you felt the most shame. That's a question this book may be repeating for you, and I hope that these reflections give you the sense that you are not alone in feeling shame. God does not want your shame to be an obstacle to knowing how much God loves you and wants you to live in the certain knowledge that you are God's beloved.

No, by asking where do you feel shame, I mean, where *in your body* do you feel shame? Emotions are not ideas; they do not limit themselves to the synapses of the brain. At the same time, ideas can evoke emotions. It's hard to imagine that Einstein did not experience a kind of euphoria when striking upon one of the most elevated ideas of the last century, the general theory of relativity. We know how excited we can get when an idea dawns upon us. We know how we can be physically relieved when we remember a name we thought was long lost. Ideas, concepts, theories, activities of the brain can generate feelings. And certain emotions are attached to different places in our bodies.

For instance, I feel fear and stress—they are usually interwoven—in my chest. My pulse quickens and my breathing becomes more shallow and rapid. In contrast, a colleague actually finds his heart rate slowing down when he is stressed; his body is telling him to slow way down. When anger strikes, I feel it on my scalp, as though I am being electrically charged. Sadness opens a cavern deep in my gut. Though it feels like an empty space, I lose my appetite and experience an urge to double over and collapse.

Though shame can sometimes bring all of these feelings at once, they are joined by weakness, a kind of faltering or frailty right behind my eyes. It's hard to even look at anything. I just want to enter a dark space, to hide, to neither see nor be seen. Remember the description of the character portrayed by Buster Keaton in Samuel Beckett's foray into cinema entitled *Film* from chapter 1? When attacked or enveloped by shame, I am that man! Buster Keaton, *c'est moi*.

Blindness

Remarkably, there appears to be plenty of literary, scriptural, and artistic precedent for making a link between the emotion of shame and the eyes. How can we forget the instinctive reaction of Oedipus in the ancient play cycle by Sophocles after he realizes that he has been in an incestuous marriage with his mother and he has killed his own father? Upon seeing the dead body of Jocaste, his mother, after her suicide, he takes the pin from the brooch of her gown and gouges out his own eyes. In the book of Genesis, the first consequence of Adam and Eve's fall is not a slap on the wrist or a verbal chastisement. No, the effect of their sin is realized by the opening of their eyes. It's not the fact that they can see that is harmful; rather it is what they see that hurts: themselves as creatures who are infinitely separate from God. Shame distorts how we see who we are in relation to God and by extension to the world itself. Shame wants to blind us.

One of the most powerful depictions of shame's blindness can be found on the walls of a church in Florence, Italy. In the Brancacci Chapel in the Church of Santa Maria del Carmine, the artist Masaccio rendered the *Expulsion of Adam and Eve from Eden* in the fifteenth century. The fresco is the image of shame. Adam's head is lowered, both his hands covering his face. One can almost feel his right thumb on the corner of his eye and his left hand adding another layer of darkness as he crosses the threshold from the Garden into a barren and rocky landscape. Eve's eyes are closed and her mouth is like an open gash from which we can virtually hear a wail, a howl of grief. Her hands and arms cover her breasts and genitalia. Adam's gestures seek to prevent him from seeing. Eve strives not to be seen. Shame blinds. Masaccio took some liberty with the Genesis text. Rather than covering up the couple with fig leaf aprons, he chose to render the emotional and spiritual effect of shame as it strikes Adam and Eve *in their bodies*. Their ability to see is so affected by the awareness of their separation from God so as to make them long for blindness. It seems they share this longing with characters from as far back as Oedipus to as recent as Samuel Beckett's O, portrayed by Buster Keaton.

The fresco is paired in the Brancacci Chapel with the image of our primeval parents in tranquility, surrounded by lush and deep green. This fresco is done by another Renaissance artist, Masolino da Panicale. In this depiction, though we see the serpent at the moment of temptation, the couple seem much more serene. It is the moment before the Fall from Grace; Eve has the fruit in her hand, yet she has not yet partaken of it nor has she offered it to her partner. If we spend a few minutes studying the faces of our parents in this earlier scene, we might come to the conclusion they also are blind, though not from shame. Their faces are utterly blank, expressionless. They gaze at each other without curiosity or any expression of appreciation for the other. The words one might use to describe the expression in their eyes are hollow, vacant, empty. What do they see?

Both artists, Masaccio (a nickname meaning "Big Thomas") and Masolino ("Little Thomas"), make statements about what it means to be human in the sight of God. Masolino seems to be saying that Adam and Eve, in having a relationship with God before the experience of separation, don't know how good they have it. The vacancy of their eyes and the blankness of their expressions convey the emotionless inner world. Though their surroundings are lush, verdant, and serene, they display no character or personality. One is led to question that if "ignorance is bliss," how can we know bliss if we've not experienced its opposite, that is, suffering?

In contrast, Masaccio's fresco of the fallen Adam and Eve shows character. These are real human beings with whom we can identify, however uncomfortably. They are racked with pain. Their inner life and the depth of their shame are shown physically. Even though they are being expelled into a barren landscape with no sign of vegetation or life, they have come alive to the viewer in their agony. Shame may instill in them a yearning to be blind, but these are people we recognize. Indeed, at times we may recognize them, if we are honest with ourselves, when we look in the mirror, read the newspaper, watch the evening news, or log on to Facebook.

Recall the first effect of Adam and Eve's disobedience. Their eyes are opened. But what did they see? Their first sight upon eating from the tree of the knowledge is that they are separate from God. They see an infinite chasm between themselves and the one from whom they had, until then, no reason or cause to see themselves as separate. The sight of themselves as essentially isolated and separate from God, the source of their being, instantaneously leads them to a comparison with God that results in the experience of shame. Shame can, in a real sense, be defined as the inner pain that stems from the deep reckoning of one's ultimate and irrefutable limitation.

There is something about shame that is powerfully self-annihilating. The fig leaves can be thought of as the most immediate and only means available to our ancestors not only to be hidden, but to be undifferentiated from the trees among which they walk. It's not too much of a stretch to suggest that by donning the fig leaves, Adam and Eve seek to disappear, to say to themselves and each other, and quite possibly to God, "I am so separate from the One Who Is that I am not." Understood in this way, shame wants to convince us that we are better off not being seen because the burden of being seen for who shame wants to convince us we are—wretched, loathsome, irreparably broken—is intolerable. Remember the terror in Buster Keaton's eyes in Samuel Beckett's *Film*.

Sight

Into this wide range of meaning of our fall from grace enters the writer of the Gospel of John. There can be no doubt that John the Evangelist is not only familiar with the book of Genesis but also drenched in its literary subtleties. John's storytelling depends on the storytelling in Genesis. Sure, we could read the Fourth Gospel without having read Genesis or Exodus, but our appreciation of Christ's taking on our human flesh, suffering, dying, and rising again would be much less liberating from the effects of shame and fear if we just read it without seeing the previous narratives. From the very opening verses of the gospel to the scene in the garden where Mary Magdalene's eyes are opened to recognize Jesus, whom she initially fails to recognize, thinking him to be a gardener, John relies on the earlier books of the Bible.

John the Evangelist deliberately chooses to begin his gospel with the same words that open the Bible: *In the beginning*. As the book of Genesis begins to tell the story of creation and humankind's relationship with God, John retells the story, adding a new layer of meaning and opening new possibilities in the Word-made-flesh. Read in this way, it becomes possible to see our primeval parents reappear in the presence of their God, who is not at all satisfied with their expulsion and their disgrace.

One of the most elaborately detailed and intricate parallels between the first book of the Bible and the Fourth Gospel occurs in the story of the man who is blind from birth. As we read the ninth chapter of John, almost every detail of Jesus' encounters with this fascinating character, from his first meeting, to his being "christened" with mud, to the man's curious expulsion out of the presence of the religious authorities, serves as an echo of the story of Adam's distortion of sight and consequent expulsion from Paradise.

With all this in the background, John the Evangelist tells the story of Jesus' opening the eyes of a man who was blind from birth. Just as Adam represents both our first parent and all humanity, so the unnamed man who is blind from his genesis represents anyone who is unable to recognize their worth and dignity in God's eyes. The man, blind from birth, gives us a marvelous background to one of the earliest prayers in the Book of Common Prayer:

> O God, who wonderfully created, and yet more wonderfully restored, the dignity of human nature: Grant that we may share the divine life of him who humbled himself to share our humanity, your Son Jesus Christ; who lives and reigns with you, in the unity of the Holy Spirit, one God, for ever and ever. (Collect of the Second Sunday after Christmas Day, and of the Incarnation, 214)

John tells how the story of Jesus gives us back our vision in some remarkable ways—ways that are just plain fun to notice in a careful reading, especially if one has the story of Adam and Eve's fall close at hand. The actual healing of the man born blind takes only two short verses to describe. After referring to himself as the light of the world, Jesus:

> spat on the ground and made mud with the saliva and spread the mud on the man's eyes, saying to him, "Go, wash in the pool of Siloam" (which means Sent). Then he went and washed and came back able to see. (John 9:6–7)

But the whole story is much more textured and layered with meaning. Let me try to point out the parallels and the contrasts that would lead one to see how the Evangelist lifts this story of one man's healing into the story of restoration of all humanity's vision from shame to dignity.

Eden Restored

The first clue we have that John is making a reference to Adam and Eve is the simple action of the characters, the "blocking" as those who have had experience on stage would say. Who seeks whom? First, we have the phrase that echoes one found in the Genesis story. Jesus is walking along, just like God, who is walking in the garden in the cool of the evening, looking for God's beloved creatures. It's not the blind man that is first seeking the Son of God, but God who seeks the blind.

Another curious suggestion that the man represents more than an individual can be found in the phrase "man who was blind from birth." In the simple "street Greek" that was the original language in which John wrote, the phrase certainly says that the man is born with an ocular disability. But the word used for "from birth" is linked in its root to the same word for "the beginning," that is, "from genesis." Biblical scholars may accuse me of stretching this a bit, but so be it. In other words, the man Jesus encounters when he walks along is the man whose eyes have been closed since the original human beings, Adam and Eve.

Like so many figures whom Jesus heals, raises, feeds, and forgives in the New Testament, this man has no name. He can, therefore, be *any* man, *every human* who shares the same fallen, impaired condition that the story of Adam and Eve explains and depicts. He is both Adam and Eve. This unnamed figure (whom some scholars describe as one of the most fascinating characters in all the Gospels)—the man blind from the beginning—can stand for you and me. Lest the reader think I'm reading too much into this fascinating and detailed story, it's worth citing the fourth-century bishop and theologian Augustine, who said:

> If we reflect, then, on what is signified by the deed here done, that blind man is the human race; for this blindness had place in the first man, through sin, from whom we all draw our origin, not only in respect of death, but also of unrighteousness. (Augustine, *Tractates on the Gospel of John*, Tractate 44)

When God discovers Adam and Eve in the garden, God poses a question about the origin of their new condition of shame. Seeing that they are hiding themselves from God behind their fig leaves— one might say they have invented the first articles of camouflage as they seek cover in what hunters in New Hampshire might call a tree blind—God asks, "Who told you that you were naked?" It's a question that seeks to get to the root of their newfound spiritual state.

Likewise, Jesus asks a question that is not identical but is certainly related to the one God asks in the Garden of Eden. The question gets not only to the condition of the man's eyes, but more pointedly to his spiritual state. Jesus asks, "Who sinned, this man or his parents?" When one reads the whole chapter in which this healing story is told, including the later interactions with the religious authorities whom Jesus accuses of being blind in their unacknowledged sin, Jesus could just as easily have asked, "Are Adam and Eve his parents?" or "Who told you that you were blind?" It's not a condition of the lenses, retina, or the optic nerve that this story seems to be about.

I AM

When I consider my own experience of shame, or when I examine the faces of the Masaccio fresco or the panicked face of Keaton in the Beckett film, I encounter the instinct to disappear, to hide from myself, from others, even from God. If shame says, "I wish not to be," its opposite would be, "I am here. I exist. I share in this colossal, ineffable thing called Being."

And this is precisely what happens to the man "blind from the beginning." The man is transfigured by Jesus' anointing, from being consigned merely to eek out a hollow subsistence to having his dignity restored as one who is himself "christened." Not even Lazarus, who is called out from three days of death, is bestowed upon by the evangelist the phrase of central significance in John's Gospel, the God-revealing phrase, I AM.

This I AM, repeated throughout the Gospel of John, is a reference to God's revelation to Moses at the burning bush in the book of Exodus. At the moment of Moses' calling to lead the people of Israel out of slavery, we read this exchange:

> But Moses said to God, "If I come to the Israelites and say to them, 'The God of your ancestors has sent me to you,' and they ask me, 'What is his name?' what shall I say to them?" God said to Moses, "I AM WHO I AM." He said further, "Thus you shall say to the Israelites, 'I AM has sent me to you.'" God also said to Moses, "Thus you shall say to the Israelites, 'The LORD, the God of your ancestors, the God of Abraham, the God of Isaac, and the God of Jacob, has sent me to you':
>
> This is my name forever, and this my title for all generations."
> (Exodus 3:13–15)

The Jesus of John's Gospel makes repeated references to this revelation of God's name and essence. The eight "I AM" statements in John's Gospel establish what many call the "high Christology" of John; that in the human being, Jesus, can also be found God's full presence and power. As Jesus asserts his divine nature in the "I AM" statements, these declarations also reveal a particular aspect of God's mission to restore humankind's intended relationship with God. There are several instances where we see this usage of I AM in connection with a description of how God is revealed in a specific way:

> I am the bread of life. (6:35, 51)
>
> I am the light of the world. (8:12; 9:5)
>
> I am the [sheep]gate. (10:7, 9)
>
> I am the good shepherd. (10:11, 14)
>
> I am the resurrection and the life. (11:25)
>
> I am the way, the truth, and the life. (14:6)
>
> I am the true vine. (15:1, 5)

There are also several places in John when Jesus displays God's power simply by asserting his existence. Two startling examples of the force of the "I AM" statements come to mind. The first is when Jesus appears to his disciples who are in a state of panic while rowing in the dark and turbulent Sea of Galilee:

> When they rowed about three or four miles, they saw Jesus walking on the sea and coming near the boat, and they were terrified. But he said to them, "I am;[14] do not be afraid." Then they wanted

---

14. The NRSV translates this sentence, "It is I." In the example that follows, John 18:6, the Greek is translated, "I am he." However, in each case the original Greek, *ego eimi*, is simply the subject and verb "I am."

to take him into the boat, and immediately the boat reached the land toward which they were going. (John 6:19–21)

Jesus' stroll on the water, far more than just a magic trick, is a disclosure of the Being of God who has authority even over the usual order of nature. John refers to these events not as miracles, but as signs, revelations of how God can "be" in the world, even our world.

Another striking example of the power of Jesus simply "being" occurs at the time of his arrest in the Garden of Gethsemane. Then, as the forces of both empire and religion have aligned against him, he is asked who he is.

> So Judas brought a detachment of soldiers together with police from the chief priests and the Pharisees, and they came there with lanterns and torches and weapons. Then Jesus, knowing all that was to happen to him, came forward and asked them, "Whom are you looking for?" They answered, "Jesus of Nazareth." Jesus answered, "I am he."[15] Judas, who betrayed him, was standing with them. When Jesus said to them, "I am," they stepped back and fell to the ground. (John 18:3–6)

The staggering of this contingent is such a peculiar detail that seems so hard to comprehend during the usual reading of the Passion on Good Friday, even when the passage is divided into dramatic parts. What kind of agency or power of a person, upon simply stating that he or she exists, would cause a detachment, a whole battalion of soldiers, police, and religious authorities, to stumble backward and fall to the ground, as though being pushed by a mighty wind? Perhaps it is indeed John's

---

15. Greek: *I am.*

intent to suggest that this is the same I AM WHO I AM that blows all night over the Red Sea, causing it to separate and form two walls between which the people of Israel pass through as though on dry land. Jesus, at his own arrest by the powers of this world, is the same I AM by whom those who trust in God can find passage to freedom.

It is hardly by accident that in just a few verses later, Peter is asked about his own relationship to Jesus, the I AM. His denial of Jesus is simultaneously a denial of himself.

> The woman said to Peter, "You are not also one of this man's disciples, are you?" He said, "I am not." (John 18:17)

The shame and indignity that result from Peter's threefold denial of his relationship with Christ around the charcoal fire in Gethsemane is reversed by the threefold affirmation of his love for the risen Jesus around the charcoal fire on the beach (John 21:15–17). There, Peter is told to tend the sheep and feed the lambs, thus sharing in the mission and identity of Jesus, who earlier stated, "I am the good shepherd."

The man born blind is the only character besides Jesus whose dignity, restored and reclaimed, empowers him to assert his being. When he keeps saying "I am" to the Pharisees when they ask him if he is the same beggar who had been blind since birth, it is with the same inner authority and strength that is displayed by Christ himself. It is not merely his eyesight that is restored to him, but the power to confront the authorities with the same inner strength and confidence that Jesus displays when arguing with the Pharisees, the Temple merchants, and even Pontius Pilate.

> The man answered, "Here is an astonishing thing! You do not know where he comes from, and yet he opened my eyes. We know

that God does not listen to sinners, but he does listen to one who worships him and obeys his will. Never since the world began has it been heard that anyone opened the eyes of a person born blind. If this man were not from God, he could do nothing." They answered him, "You were born entirely in sins, and are you trying to teach us?" And they drove him out. (John 9:30–31)

This is shame's polar opposite. The Yiddish word for this kind of confidence is *chutzpah*. It sees things for what they are, fully trusting God's steadfast presence. It is willing to risk being rejected by those who would deny God's goodness. We can say that it is shame's exact opposite.

Christenings

Neither Adam and Eve in Masaccio's fresco *Expulsion of Adam and Eve from Eden,* nor Keaton in Beckett's *Film,* display an ounce of that quality. It could be inferred that the boldness that allows the man to point out the Pharisees' hypocrisy—"Here's an astonishing thing!"—springs from the dignity conveyed to him by his being re-created in the mud "christening" by Jesus. The word translated by the NRSV "spread" is actually rooted in the same word from which we get "christ"—which means "to anoint." Christ is the Anointed One, and Jesus' mission is to restore all humankind to its intended holy status of dignity and favor. John's Gospel suggests that such boldness and freedom is a trait that comes from being "christened" by the One who fashions us out of mud and who restores us with the waters of baptism, in order to "share the divine life of the one who humbled himself by becoming human." Rather than cowering in the presence of those who refuse to see the dignity of human nature, we are invited "to be," to assert our existence, our own "I am!" and that of the oppressed, in the face of powers of domination.

The story ends with Jesus giving a kind of riddle, like a Zen koan, that leaves his hearers wondering who is blind, who can see, and whose vision is obstructed by sin or shame.

> Jesus said, "I came into this world for judgment so that those who
> do not see may see, and those who do see may become blind."
> (John 9:39)

We are among those hearers. To what extent are we blinded by our sin, that screen or covering that prevents us from seeing who we really are and that blinds us from seeing our neighbor as a child of the light?

My own blindness was revealed to me one morning in my office at the church where I served as rector. It was the day after a very exuberant and cheerful annual meeting. The spirits in the parish were high after we had just successfully completed the largest capital campaign in the church's history, allowing us to refurbish the worship space, adding accessibility and a bright, welcoming meeting space. By all the usual measures, the congregation had gotten back into the game after recovering from a period of trauma. I was riding high when I came into the office the next morning. Then there was a knock on the door. It was Muriel, a woman who, with her husband, Robert, had just started attending the parish. They were both professional people and prominent citizens in our town. The congregation and I were all delighted that they had decided to join Grace Church, and their attendance felt like a validation of the health of the parish's programs and vitality. After sitting down in my office, she began:

"Rob, I have to tell you how disappointed I am in you."

My heart sank. I felt the air from the cheery balloon of the annual meeting begin to leak.

"How so, Muriel? Tell me."

"At the annual meeting, you answered the questions of everyone who had their hand up."

"Everyone who wanted to speak had a chance to. Yes?"

"Everyone but me."

"I'm sorry, Muriel. Did you want to say something yesterday?"

"Yes, I did. I raised my hand several times."

"You did? I'm sorry. I didn't see you."

"Yes. I gathered that. But, you see, I was sitting in the front row. Just in front of you."

"I must have missed you."

"But, you see, Rob. I was the only black woman in the room. And you didn't see me?"

It's hard to describe the feeling that overcame me at that moment. Judgment. Shame. That weakening sensation in the eyes where tears gather. The urge to put my hands over my face.

Jesus said, "But now that you say, 'We see,' your sin remains." (John 9:41)

I wish I could say that the story has a happy ending. I apologized, not only for my oversight on that particular Sunday, but also for my blindness, and I thanked her for having opened my eyes to the legacy of racism that lingers in my ears and in my eyes. I offered to meet with her again. I mailed a letter expressing both my gratitude for the graceful way she said to me, "I AM!" and my remorse for not having seen or heard her. No response. Muriel and Robert stopped attending. For many Sundays, when I looked out into the pews, my eyes scanned the congregation to see if they were there. In fact, my eyes scanned looking for those I did not see before. As Martin Luther King Jr. observed, "the most segregated hour of Christian America is eleven o'clock on Sunday morning." Muriel's confrontation "christened" me to this reality, one that I can find no other word to describe but "shameful."

My interaction with Muriel ended with a separation. Though in the months and years that followed we had some civil and respectful encounters, there was still a deep awareness that true reconciliation would require hard work. The Pharisees did not seem to have much remorse or regret for having cast out the man whose sight and dignity were restored by Jesus. If anything, Muriel's meeting with me on that Monday morning opened my eyes more widely to see how far we have to go in our nation and in our church to further God's mission of reconciliation. Her ministry to me that day was a simultaneous christening into both the wounds and the light of Christ.

Questions for Reflection and Discussion

- Where, in your body, do you feel shame? What exercises or practices help you when these feelings come on? Meditation, yoga, a long walk, a session with a trusted counselor, a trip to the gym?
- Reading the story of the man born blind in John 9, is there a character with whom you identify the most strongly? What do you make of Augustine's statement that the man "stands in" for you and all humanity?
- How does the smearing, literally the "christening," of mud relate to our own baptism? Do you feel your baptism empowers you to stand up and say "I AM!" with the same authority exhibited by the man in John 9? If so, how? If not, what would be empowering to you?

6

What Appearances to Save

O God, by the passion of your blessed Son you made an instrument
of shameful death to be for us the means of life: Grant us so to glory
in the cross of Christ, that we may gladly suffer shame and loss for the
sake of your Son our Savior Jesus Christ; who lives and reigns with
you and the Holy Spirit, one God, for ever and ever. Amen.
                          —Collect for Tuesday in Holy Week, BCP, 220

Shame enslaves. Its hold on the soul can be so tight that one can hardly imagine what it's like to live free from its distortions. It tells us that freedom from its clutches is unattainable. Shame's shackles can be so integrated into our psyche that they affect all our relationships, even those that are closest to us. This may seem like a wild overstatement to many. However, when I speak of shame to many of my friends and colleagues in the Church, I discover that it is very prevalent, especially among those who, like me, grew up in families where a parent was affected by alcoholism. In such families, the reality of our humanity is too much to bear, and we are told that we must "keep up appearances" or be subject to ridicule or scorn. Some learn early on that love is not "unconditional" but depends on merit. Words of approval or expressions of love come only once one has done something to deserve them. Soon, one learns that achievement and accomplishment are what drive us because they are the only ways we can gain a sense of worth in a parent's eyes. Children in such families then learn to see God as an extension of their own alcoholic family: arbitrary, often withholding of love or affection, moody, intolerant of weakness or need, impatient of mistakes or conditions that are simply part of being human.

Scars of Shame

One of my most persistent memories of shame occurred in the waiting room of a doctor's office. I was perhaps twelve or thirteen years old and afflicted with a condition common among teenagers: acne. My face was so angry with pimples that I refused to have my photograph taken. Waiting at the school bus stop meant being exposed to the ridicule of my classmates, even those afflicted with the same disease. Often, after having his post-work scotch and water, my father would demand that I stand next to him so that he could offer his own "treatment" and squeeze the pustules on his own. I still carry the scars, and to this day the smell of scotch on another's breath causes me to flinch. His remedy proved to be ineffective, and my father acquiesced to making an appointment with a dermatologist.

We arrived and I sat down in the waiting room, where I saw people afflicted with different dermatological conditions. There was a girl about my age, with a slighter case of pimples. There was a middle-aged woman with some kind of splotches all over her cheeks. There was a man with what looked like hardened spheres, cysts of some kind, piled on his nose. Another woman wore white gloves, though it was a warm day in late summer.

My father stood at the glass window to announce our arrival for the appointment. "Robby's here to be treated for his zits," he said in a voice loud enough for all to hear. After the receptionist said that the doctor would be right with us, my father added, "You know, I don't know why he has this problem. I never had this problem when I was a kid."

As noted earlier, shame tells us it's not that you made a mistake; it's that you are a mistake. It's not that you have flaws, it's that you are a flaw. Though they have long ago ceased to cause pain or anguish, the facial scars left behind by the Scotch-inspired "treatments" and the psychic pockmarks left behind by an offhand comment in a public waiting room endure. One cannot fully erase these marks, but they can be transformed, even transfigured, into signs of how fully God accepts us even if we bear wounds. It is not by accident that the resurrected Jesus appears before his disciples, the same ones who denied and abandoned him at the foot of the cross, *with the wounds still on his hands, his side, and his feet* (see Luke 24:39).

My own marks and memories, though small in comparison to the countless who have suffered much more severe and damaging injuries, connect me to those whose experiences may not be exactly the same, but who can nonetheless sympathize with how shame enters lives at a tender age. To be clear, I have long since forgiven my father for this injury and for others. Being a parent myself now gives me a heightened sensitivity to how my own sense of insecurity and inadequacy can be visited upon my children. The awareness of how shame can be passed on from one person to another, and especially from parent to child,

92 — Without Shame or Fear

stirs deep compassion for my dad and the unspoken burdens he carried, even to his grave.

Liberation from Shame

Among the myriad meanings of the Gospel, very close to its heart is the message that in Jesus we can be liberated from the bondage of shame. Jesus comes to restore in us a sense that we are God's beloved, despite our moral failings, physical blemishes, and imperfections. In the crucified Jesus, God takes the wounds that others have inflicted upon us. Indeed, he even chooses to *become* shameful in order to transform what was considered gross and sordid into a new creation. This can be read easily in Paul's interpretation of the humiliation and death of Jesus on the cross:

> So if anyone is in Christ, there is a new creation: everything old has passed away; see, everything has become new! . . . For our sake he made him to be sin who knew no sin, so that in him we might become the righteousness of God. (2 Corinthians 5:17, 21)

If sin drives a wedge between God and us, then shame is our emotional and spiritual response to that condition of separation and degradation. Understood in this way, what Jesus does, by subjecting himself to the status of sin in the eyes of his accusers and the crowd, is represent and reflect back to us the shame we all feel, if we are at all honest about our separation from God.

The moment in the liturgical year that has come to address most directly both my shame and God's desire to liberate me from its thrall is Maundy Thursday. Every year on that night we are reintroduced to the freedom that comes from knowing that Jesus desires all of us to be washed from the encrustations of sin that make us feel so unworthy to stand before God. The message of Jesus—his teaching, his actions, his encounters with us, and above all, his passion and resurrection—shows us how God chooses to liberate us from the grip of shame. This is how I have come to approach the liturgy that opens the Triduum—the Great Three Days of Easter. Maundy Thursday, though it comes at the beginning of Easter, is just that—the inauguration of Easter. The recitation of the story of the Exodus, its connection to the Last Supper, and the action of Jesus that bridges and links the two events—these are at the heart of Christianity's meaning and relevance for all ages, especially for our age, as devoid of grace as it appears.

The washing of the disciples' feet, and the invitation to us to wash each other's feet, is the new Exodus, the new path to freedom. On Easter Day we often sing the words of this ancient hymn from the eighth-century monk and poet John of Damascus:

> Come, ye faithful raise the strain
> With triumphant gladness!
> God has brought forth Israel
> into joy from sadness,
> loosed from Pharaoh's bitter yoke
> Jacob's sons and daughters;
> led them with unmoistened foot
> through the Red Sea waters. (Hymnal 1982, #199)

On Maundy Thursday it is *with moistened feet* that we celebrate a new Exodus from our slavery to shame and disgrace to a place of honor and dignity through the power of God's total acceptance of us as God's own. That God would choose, in the gestures of tender kindness of our neighbor and our own companions in the faith, to wash our cracked and soiled feet can be the most scandalous mystery modern Christians face. Indeed, in a culture that is based on shame, to allow one's feet to be washed is more difficult and more strenuous for many of us than to make a profound bow to the cross on Good Friday. At the heart of the *missio dei*—that mission for which God has a church—is the liberation of all people from the bonds of shame.

And yet in the opinion of many Christians, it is shame—or its twin, reputation—that holds the whole church together. After all, what would happen if we were utterly free from the need to keep up appearances? Until I am liberated of my own shame, I will remain a timid bishop who leads a frozen flock. Until we let go of our need to uphold or defend a reputation of privilege, the church will remain isolated within the stone walls to which it is shackled.

Maundy Thursday

The service of Maundy Thursday interweaves two contrasting experiences of liberation, revealing two strategies by which God chooses to free God's people. The first story we hear on Maundy Thursday is from the Book of Exodus and recounts the first Passover. This story provides the context and the background for John's Gospel to describe what Jesus does with his disciples in the Upper Room. In the Exodus story, God, exasperated by the hardness of heart of Pharaoh despite Moses' repeated warnings, delivers Israel by sheer force and might. In the reading we hear on Maundy Thursday, the first Passover is explained in this way:

> For I will pass through the land of Egypt that night, and I will strike down every firstborn in the land of Egypt, both human

beings and animals; on all the gods of Egypt I will execute judg-
ments: I am the LORD. The blood shall be a sign for you on the
houses where you live: when I see the blood, I will pass over you,
and no plague shall destroy you when I strike the land of Egypt.

This day shall be a day of remembrance for you. You shall
celebrate it as a festival to the LORD; throughout your generations
you shall observe it as a perpetual ordinance. (Exodus 12:12–14)

God's people are to remember how God has acted, and how God,
being God, is at liberty to act—with force, violence, and power that
can destroy and cause tremendous suffering, even if it results in the
deliverance of those who live under brutal oppression.

The readings of Maundy Thursday can be disorienting in how they
present starkly contrasting stories of how God can choose to act. The
story of the first Passover and the Deliverance at the Red Sea is one
that portrays a God who is capable of entering the field of both human
and natural events in a way that overwhelms an oppressive military
power. Only a few minutes later in the service, we hear the story of
God, in Jesus, choosing a drastically different means to free us from
what oppresses us. This contrast has caused many through the ages to
deny that the God of the Hebrew Bible is the same God as the God
of the New Testament. The former acts with "shock and awe," the
latter with gentleness and humility and is incapable of behaving with
any kind of violence. The Church's teaching has always rejected this
splitting of God, and here, quite possibly, is the reason why: If Jesus
does not have a choice to call down the heavenly hosts and legions to
eliminate by force all of God's opponents, then his service at the feet of
his disciples is not an exercise of freedom that we ourselves are invited
to share.

As we contrast this mode of liberation with what is displayed in the Upper Room, it is essential that we preserve an understanding of God's ultimate sovereignty and freedom. By describing the Upper Room story we hear later in the Maundy Thursday liturgy, we are not meant to dis- avow the "God of the Old Testament" as though we are talking about two different Gods—one of violence and wrath, and one of meekness and humility. God's expressions of loving kindness, humility, and ser- vanthood would all be meaningless and devoid of effect if they were not the result of a choice. If God were not capable of choosing to share our humanity, our suffering, and our shame, then God's actions would be akin to the actions of a slave or the victim of abuse. The actions of servility themselves may bring some short-lived and hollow benefit to the oppressor, but they cannot in any way be construed as motivated by love—fear, shame, or control, perhaps, but never love. Indeed, the actions certainly increase the guilt of the one who oppresses.

In comparing the ways that God's actions are recounted on Maundy Thursday, we must caution against the attitude that says that Jesus is "superseding" the God of the Exodus. We are not saying that God is not free to act with the same drama and even violence seen before. God is not constrained to behave like a slave. Rather God chooses to limit God's force in order to show us a new way—a new departure from our shame—so that our whole selves, including our bodies, can be made acceptable to God (Romans 12:1).

Vulnerability

In Jesus Christ, God chooses to act nonviolently in order to bring about God's Realm in human society. In a sense, God's reputation as all- powerful, in control, always pure and ritually clean is on the line in the events of Holy Week. Stupendously and in a way that will always befuddle the powers of the world, God chooses to put down that reputation in order to rise victorious over all that oppresses us, including shame and the fear of death.

Thus, it is out of God's own freedom and choice, and out of God's own desire to liberate and restore our relationship with God and each other, that we learn of the "mind of Christ" as Jesus gathers the disciples for the Passover meal on the night of his arrest:

> Now before the festival of the Passover, Jesus knew that his hour had come to depart from this world and go to the Father. Having loved his own who were in the world, he loved them to the end. The devil had already put it into the heart of Judas son of Simon Iscariot to betray him. And during supper Jesus, knowing that the Father had given all things into his hands, and that he had come from God and was going to God, got up from the table, took off his outer robe, and tied a towel around himself. Then he poured water into a basin and began to wash the disciples' feet and to wipe them with the towel that was tied around him. (John 13:1–5)

It is hard to see how John could be any more explicit or direct in making the connection between Israel's "departure" from slavery in Egypt and Jesus' "departure" from the world. Now, in this passage, John is making an even more dramatic and startling link. Prior to the ritual Passover meal that recounts God's slaying of all the firstborn of Egypt as well as the drowning of Pharaoh's legions in the Red Sea, is the astonishing contrast of Jesus' disrobing and kneeling before his followers. This juxtaposition has the effect of expanding how we are to understand divine power in the light of the resurrection. The freedom to serve in such a subservient and humble manner is derived from Jesus' profound awareness that he has *already,* even before the crucifixion and resurrection, been "given all things into his hands." Shame can gain no purchase when one has such an awareness of oneself or one's neighbor.

Cosmos

The "departure from this world" implies more than Jesus' physical death and entrance into a realm beyond this earth. In John's language, whenever Jesus uses the term "world" (the Greek word is *cosmos*), he appears to refer not merely to life on this planet, but rather to the whole matrix of relationships, attitudes, tendencies, and habits that work contrary to the movement of God. This understanding of John's use of the word "world" is what so many countless Christians through the ages have grasped when they quote what Martin Luther called the "Gospel in a nutshell."[16]

> For God so loved the world that he gave his only Son, so that everyone who believes in him may not perish but have eternal life. (John 3:16)

We are not to understand this condensed gospel-in-one-verse as a ringing endorsement of the world as we know it. Though God astonishingly gives such tender regard to the "cosmos," the world remains a realm where God's children are in peril of death. The surrender of God's Son into the fallen world is how God grants us access to the grace of God that leads to life. In the context of the Passover meal, Jesus is said to be deeply aware of his own departure from this world. Rather than plotting an armed or political coup of all the powers of

---

16. *Luther's Works* 35:118.

domination, represented by either military occupation (the Romans) or religious shame (the Temple authorities, the Pharisees), Jesus chooses instead to show his followers how we can remain in the world to further God's mission in transforming it.

The new Exodus, the departure from the degrading powers of the world, takes place with the moistened feet of the Jesus followers who are invited, not forced, to do likewise to those in the fallen *cosmos*. In this way, knowing that the resurrection is already ours, and that in Christ all things have been given into our hands, God chooses the Church to further the mission of reconciliation, healing, and peace.

Blessings, Wounds, and Exfoliation

It's been said that every preacher essentially has one sermon. I hope that's not true. With all due respect to the great reformer, Martin Luther, the Gospel is just too loaded with meanings to be reduced to one sermon, let alone one verse. The mission of God in Jesus Christ is simply uncontainable. The disciple who claims authorship of the Fourth Gospel states as much:

> But there are also many other things that Jesus did; if every one of them were written down, I suppose that the world itself could not contain the books that would be written. (John 21:25)

That being said, I have to confess that my own point of contact with Jesus, the place where I feel He reaches me the most profoundly, is in the experience of shame, both as I have experienced it, and as others have shared it with me in their struggle with its complex power to damage us when we are in its thrall, and in its positive capacity, at certain times, to drive us to seek reconciliation and healing. Perhaps like the

Jacob who spent a whole night wrestling with an angel and refused to let the stranger go, I have come to wonder if my own wrestling with shame has resulted in both blessing and curse.

This strange mix of being both wounded and blessed by shame is almost never as immediate and obvious than it is at the moment of the foot washing on Maundy Thursday. To watch the faces of the people whose feet are being washed, or to be aware of the tensing of my jaw and face when my own feet are being washed, is the embodiment of the etymological ambiguity of the word blessing. The word shares a root with the old English *bletsian,* which is derived from the word *blod.* One can surmise that a blessing is connected to a sacrifice involving the shedding of blood. In French, a linguistic cousin of our own language, the word *blesser* means "to wound." Suddenly, it makes more sense that when one makes the sign of the cross upon oneself or others, one is simultaneously reminded of the passion and death of Jesus on the cross, not as a means of inflicting a wound so much as to connect one's own life with the cross of Christ, attaching our own suffering to Jesus' so that we may share in the ultimate benefit, blessing, of his rising. All this meaning is intimately intertwined with the foot washing.

To be honest, I experience a small measure of inner turmoil—I hesitate to call it agony—when I remove my shoes and socks and offer my feet to a brother or sister in Christ. It makes no difference if that companion in the faith is a dear and trusted friend or colleague, an acolyte, or a relative stranger to the Church on that evening service before Good Friday. What I feel is my own pride, my need to be perfect, scent-free, clean, sinless, without reproach. All this is blessed in the deepest sense of the word—it is assaulted and drowned in the stainless steel pan that we use for this sacrifice of praise and thanksgiving for God's love of humanity, even human flesh.

It might help to imagine that those little pieces of black lint, the product of a day in a sweaty shoe, which my friend-in-Christ washes off my toes' cuticles, represent the dead Egyptian soldiers who were left floating facedown in the Red Sea. But that crass mental trick only trivializes the real slaying that this liturgy is designed to realize: that of my pride and its need to uphold an appearance and reputation that my shame demands I present to the world. I cringe when my feet are washed because there's something in me that rails against being exposed so closely as human, flawed, imperfect, and a direct descendant of Adam and Eve. The foot washing is a sloughing of the fig leaves that have become more than a detachable accessory to my apparel but an internalized apparatus of my soul, functioning to keep the neighbor at my feet and my Savior at a safe distance. Sloughing is not always the light exfoliation provided at the spa—it can make one wince.

At the first foot washing, Peter himself winces. He initially refuses the gesture from his teacher, master, and Lord.

> He came to Simon Peter, who said to him, "Lord, are you going to wash my feet?" Jesus answered, "You do not know now what I am doing, but later you will understand." Peter said to him, "You will never wash my feet." Jesus answered, "Unless I wash you, you have no share with me." (John 13:6–8)

The reversal of roles seems too disruptive of the way the world works. It's supposed to be the servants or the students who are to wash the feet of the superior or the teacher. We can understand Peter's strong objection to this new and peculiar initiative of Jesus, whose disrobing to kneel and wash his students' feet upturns the economy; that is, the "house rules." We don't allow the master to wash anyone's feet. This is not how the world works. How shameful.

Jesus' response is even more threatening to the *cosmos*. "Unless I wash you, you have no share with me." This statement is not a mere offhand retort to Peter's objection. Jesus is not engaging in the usual etiquette we practice when opening a door—"No, please, allow me. You first." Far more than that, Jesus is showing his disciples how God's mission is to be enacted in the world. We are to allow Jesus to see and love us, bunions, lint, calluses, fungi, and all, and we are to see and love our neighbor in the same way. In other words, Jesus seems to be saying that "unless you do this, you will have no part of me. Indeed, unless you realize the power of love demonstrated in this action, you will not be a part of my body. You cannot share in the glory of the resurrection. You will not experience the triumph of God's love that can dissolve your shame in this cleansing water."

The meaning of Jesus' warning must have hit Peter so directly that he, the impetuous man whom we have come to know, responds, "Lord, not my feet only but also my hands and my head!" (John 13:9). Clearly, Peter gets it. The foot washing in the Upper Room at the Passover is more than a cleansing of the dust and grime of the streets in Jerusalem, but also removes whatever might separate him from the life that Jesus has displayed in his signs and that he has promised to those who follow him.

How curious, and perhaps even jarring, that Jesus then refrains from washing Peter's hands and head as he so enthusiastically demands. Peter's offering his whole body to be washed at that moment sounds like the buoyant request of a young convert to the faith who would not be satisfied with a mere sprinkling at the font for baptism, but wants a full immersion in the local lake. Jesus' response is measured, calm, and can be heard as a tender defense of Peter's dignity, as if to say, "Peter, you are not as lost as you think you are. Let go of your shame."

And as he continues, Jesus will suggest that there are others who are more lost, more in peril, than Peter is. Attention turns from Peter toward another, Judas. Could it be that in Peter and in Judas, we have examples of how shame can function? In the case of Peter, shame can lead one closer to the reconciling acceptance of Jesus. But Judas is the story of shame's triumph over the soul, preventing him from seeking forgiveness. The contrast between the two is heartbreaking. Peter irrationally throws his clothes on before jumping out of a boat to swim to share a joyful meal on the beach; Judas disappears, becomes lost, even annihilated—just as shame would have it.

Dissolution

I do not claim that all sense of shame is dissolved every time I share in a Maundy Thursday service foot washing. But something of it is at least partly dissolved. The wincing, the cringing at having my feet washed, is relieved almost immediately upon the reversing of roles, when I stand up, take a towel, and wash the feet of the next one in line. Over the decades of Maundy Thursday services I've learned that the condition of the feet is of less concern than the condition of the soul, the spirit, of the person whose feet I am washing. Can they allow this to take place? Is there an injury that I, the one who is pouring water over his instep, have caused over the past year that needs to be addressed? Are there amends to be made? Has Jesus called these two persons to this chair, to this particular basin, for a reason this year? Or have we played it safe, limiting the participants of the service to an appointed few?

Each time we share in the Maundy Thursday service, I feel that God is taking off one more part of the armor that has vainly served to prevent God to see me and to heal me of shame. Every time I sit in that chair and cringe as I extend my foot, what I am feeling is the crumbling of a part of the barrier between my neighbor and me. Each time that happens, I see more and more the face of Jesus.

The restoration of God's image from the damaging and distorting effects of shame might take years. It takes place in the liturgy. It takes place across coffee tables in offices when we share the struggles of God's people who have been burdened by sin, failure, or disappointments. It takes place when dreams die and reality intrudes and we are reintroduced to the God who says simply, I AM. It takes place when we discover that God is what is and that we are not meant to be alone in our weakness. Shame would have us remain alone, in isolation. God calls us to companionship.

All this is work, but as a friend in ministry used to tell me, "It is sweet work." Well, mostly. Sometimes it is bittersweet. But it is the work Jesus calls us to.

Jesus said, "Unless I wash you, you have no share with me." The mission of God brings the world to the love of Jesus, a love that dissolves shame in the waters of forgiveness. Ours is a world, a *cosmos,* motivated by shame. We can be driven to hide our light under its bushel basket of timidity or we can seek to cover it over with layers of good appearances and reputation. Jesus urges us to release the captives of shame through such acts of fundamental acceptance as washing another's feet, feeding, forgiving, seeing another whom the world refuses to acknowledge.

The poet W.H. Auden once wrote (in a poem that has a lot to do with the dissolving effects of water), "The blessed do not care what angle they are regarded from, having nothing to hide."[17]

---

17. W.H. Auden, "In Praise of Limestone," 1948.

How freeing and delightful it would be to be so blessed, to live without concern about our appearances, reputation, or shame. But the truth is, what Jesus said about the poor applies equally to shame—it will always be with us. And like the poor, we can either choose to ignore shame's place in our souls and allow it to fester and damage. Or, by the grace of the One whose own appearance was marred and disfigured, who emptied himself of all majesty and dignity on the cross, we can meet Jesus there, and allow him to raise us, yet again, and however incrementally, to the glorious liberty he desires to give to all.

"Friday's Child" is a poem Auden wrote in memory of Dietrich Bonhoeffer, certainly one of those saints who came not to care about the angle from which he was regarded, having nothing to hide, even in his martyrdom by the Gestapo just before the end of World War II. The poem ends in a way that seems fitting as a conclusion to this meditation on shame and the extent to which God has gone to free us from its clutches.

> Meanwhile, a silence on the cross,
> As dead as we shall ever be,
> Speaks of some total gain or loss,
> And you and I are free
>
> To guess from the insulted face
> Just what Appearances He saves
> By suffering in a public place
> A death reserved for slaves.[18]

---

18. W.H. Auden, "Friday's Child," 1958.

Questions for Reflection and Discussion

- This chapter compares two actions of God that lead to deliverance: the drowning of Pharaoh's army at the Red Sea and Jesus' foot washing at the Last Supper. Both stories are recounted on Maundy Thursday. What do you make of the contrast between these two actions of God to free God's people? How is one freed while choosing to serve?

- What range of thoughts and feelings have you experienced at a foot washing, or when serving others?

- What appearances or reputation do you feel compelled to save and hold onto?

- What reputation does your local church feel compelled to protect?

- What do you need to lay aside in order to serve others with the freedom from shame or fear Jesus exhibits?

CONCLUSION

Back to the Garden

If anyone is in Christ, there is a new creation.

—2 Corinthians 5:17

The Department of Corrections refers to them as the General Population. They represent a wide range of criminal activity: petty theft, larceny, burglary, domestic violence, sexual assault, drug dealing. They are either nearing the completion of their sentences or they have been deemed to represent minimum physical threat to correctional officers, to each other, or visitors from the outside.

I get to visit them in the Interfaith Chapel at least twice during the year, always for Easter. Their choir, accompanied by an electronic keyboard and a guitar, sings "Jesus Christ is risen today, Alleluia" and

> He is risen, he is risen!
> Tell it out with joyful voice:
> he has burst his three days' prison;
> let the whole wide earth rejoice;

death is conquered,

we are free, Christ has won the victory.[19]

The Gospel reading is from John 20, where we hear of the perplexing encounter between the heartbroken Mary Magdalene and the Risen Jesus at the empty tomb. While weeping and confused about the absence of the Savior's body:

> . . . she turned around and saw Jesus standing there, but she did not know that it was Jesus. Jesus said to her, "Woman, why are you weeping? Whom are you looking for?" Supposing him to be the gardener, she said to him, "Sir, if you have carried him away, tell me where you have laid him, and I will take him away." Jesus said to her, "Mary!" She turned and said to him in Hebrew, "Rabbouni!" (which means Teacher). (John 20:14–16)

It gets me every time I read this Gospel in this setting. After lowering the book, I look out at the several dozen members of this particular congregation of inmates. The prison uniform for the General Population consists of forest green work pants and shirts, each with their name on a white strip over the chest pocket. They wear work boots. They are dressed like a crew of landscapers, greenhouse workers. For the entire world, they look like gardeners to me.

We began looking at shame by remembering what happened in a garden with the first gardeners, Adam and Eve. Now here is Jesus, whom Mary Magdalene, the first real apostle, takes at first to be a gardener. And here they are, a group of men who, though incarcerated for their crimes, do not have to come to this service, but show up

---

19. Hymnal 1982, #180. Words: Cecil Francis Alexander.

nonetheless to be reminded of their having been joined with Jesus in his resurrection.

And there I am, dressed in white brocade and a mitre, straining to tell about how God does not want us to be imprisoned in our sins or burdened by our shame for past deeds. All that comes out of my constricted throat is that for all I know, God's grace has not only forgiven them, but that they themselves represent the risen Christ to me on this Easter weekend. Did not our Savior say as much when he told his disciples that when we visit those in prison, we can actually expect to meet him there, too? *As you visited these you visited me* (Matthew 25). Jesus is not afraid to go to those places the world casts in the mire of shame, places like a state or federal penitentiary.

Do not get me wrong. I would not want to trade places with my incarcerated brothers or sisters. But why is it that I come away from those Easter services, year after year, wishing I could trade in the expensive vestments that sometimes cover up who I really am for their green work clothes? I, too, am a member of the general population we call humanity. I'd like to imagine myself, if just for the duration of Easter day, as the gardener who could liberate a burdened soul like Magdalene's just by seeing her for who she is—a child of God, made a new creation by God's love.

The prisoners who sing of Christ's bursting the three days' prison convert me every time I visit them. No, they are not all of them particularly gentle or kind men. I do not hold romantic or naive notions about them. But with all the outside and cultural signs of dignity, worth, and liberty deprived them, they depend on little but an assurance of God's love to uphold them. They know something of shame, a shame I would be horrified to face. As a result, they may also know something of God's desire to redeem and restore them as a member of Christ in whose fellowship and Body our sins and our shame are washed away. This is the same Jesus who became a prisoner, even on death row, so that we may be made worthy to stand before God, forgiven, healed, renewed.

We began this investigation of shame in a garden. Even though it's in the confines of a prison, it seems fitting that we end among gardeners, made newly green by God's death-destroying and shame-dissolving grace. May we hear the voice of Jesus call us each by name and, without shame or fear, rejoice to behold his appearing.

A. Robert Hirschfeld
Feast of St. Mary Magdalene, 2016